SUCCEEDING AS A FEMALE SUPERINTENDENT

How to Get There and Stay There

**Suzanne L. Gilmour and
Mary P. Kinsella**

Published in partnership with the
American Association of School Administrators

Rowman & Littlefield Education
Lanham • New York • Toronto • Plymouth, UK

Published in partnership with
the American Association of School Administrators

Published in the United States of America
by Rowman & Littlefield Education
A division of Rowman & Littlefield Publishers, Inc.
A wholly owned subsidiary of
The Rowman & Littlefield Publishing Group, Inc.
4501 Forbes Boulevard, Suite 200, Lanham, Maryland 20706
www.rowmaneducation.com

Estover Road
Plymouth PL6 7PY
United Kingdom

British Library Cataloguing in Publication Information Available

Library of Congress Cataloging-in-Publication Data

Gilmour, Suzanne Lyness
  Succeeding as a female superintendent : how to get there and stay there /
Suzanne L. Gilmour and Mary P. Kinsella.
    p. cm.
  "Published in partnership with the American Association of School
Administrators."
  ISBN-13: 978-1-57886-925-1 (cloth : alk. paper)
  ISBN-10: 1-57886-925-0 (cloth : alk. paper)
  ISBN-13: 978-1-57886-926-8 (pbk. : alk. paper)
  ISBN-10: 1-57886-926-9 (pbk. : alk. paper)
  eISBN-13: 978-1-57886-927-5
  eISBN-10: 1-57886-927-7
  1. School superintendents—United States. 2. Women school
administrators—United States. I. Kinsella, Mary P., 1951– II. Title.
LB2831.72.G52 2009
371.2'011—dc22   2008029001

∞™ The paper used in this publication meets the minimum requirements of
American National Standard for Information Sciences—Permanence of Paper
for Printed Library Materials, ANSI/NISO Z39.48-1992.
Manufactured in the United States of America.

We dedicate this book to our mothers, Elizabeth and Gertrude, for their mentoring and their belief in us as leaders.

CONTENTS

FOREWORD

This book has long been coming. For those who care about attracting talented leaders to the superintendency, this is a "must-read." For those who care about encouraging women to the superintendency, this is a "must-read." For those who are curious about the barriers and gatekeepers of the school superintendency, *Succeeding as a Female Superintendent: How to Get There and Stay There* is a "must-read."

Authors Gilmour and Kinsella have crafted an owner's manual for the superintendency that provides essential insights to getting the job and keeping it. The authors have drawn from personal experiences in the superintendency and in the search process to get there. Their research of successful women in the top school leadership positions highlights the successes and pitfalls of the journey to the top. Gilmour and Kinsella point out that in 1930, 28 percent of the superintendents were women. In 2008, 22 percent are women. What has happened? When one places in context that 50 percent of the students in our classrooms are female, we realize the compelling need to see our school leadership match the gender balance in our classrooms.

This book makes a powerful statement to all of us who care about ascendancy to this complex role and offers many valuable guideposts for artful and inspired leadership. Our profession is greatly benefited by this enlightened assessment of the work all superintendents do—and particularly women superintendents. This book should be required reading for all students of the superintendency, school superintendents, school board members, and search consultants.

There are many lessons learned here, with the potential to be passed on to those school superintendents of the future. School leaders of the twenty-first century face a mighty task. How better to prepare these school leaders than by providing them with factual accounts of current successful school superintendents. Women and men both can reap the benefits of the lessons learned and shared in this book by these successful women superintendents. It is an easy read and a "must-read." Well done!

Sarah Jerome, Ed.D.
President, American Association of School Administrators (AASA)
Superintendent of Schools (former)

ACKNOWLEDGMENTS

We gratefully acknowledge the contributions from women superintendents across New York State who talked with us, answered our questions, shared their triumphs and frustrations, and graciously let us into their professional and personal lives. Some superintendents met with us on more than one occasion and all openly shared their wisdom, understanding, and multitude of experiences. Their willingness to pass on what they have learned to the next generation of school leaders and their trust in us to tell their stories were invaluable to the completion of this book.

In particular, Kathleen M. Wood, superintendent of the Harpursville Central School District in Harpursville, New York, contributed extensively to our chapter on budgeting basics and offered tips in other sections as well. As a former school business official, her knowledge and expertise were critical in accurately portraying that portion of the superintendent's work.

We would like to acknowledge the support from faculty members Dr. William Silky and Dr. James Merrins. We would also like to thank former superintendent and author Suzanne Tingley for her editing and clarifying. We would like to thank members of the New York State Association for Women in Administration for their willingness to participate in this study and to provide valuable networking for us. In particular, Suzanne would like to thank her writing mentor, Barbara A. Roberts. Additionally, Mary would like to recognize Dr. Marilyn Tallerico, who first inspired her to do research on the superintendency.

And, most importantly, we are grateful for the love and support of our families and friends. Without their constancy in each of our lives, this book would still be just a dream! Thank you all!

❶

OVERVIEW

Mary was ready to take the step into the superintendency, or so she thought. She had taught students in physical education at all grade levels and coached at the varsity level for fifteen years, all the while advancing her learning through both public and private universities. All she had left to do was write and defend her doctoral dissertation and she would have achieved another one of her professional life goals.

A retired district superintendent of a Regional Educational Center, who was now working at a university, had mentored Mary while she worked on the research for her dissertation. In the course of their relationship, he had introduced her throughout the state to numerous powerful people, some of whom wielded great influence in school districts' searches for new superintendents. Mary never really pictured herself as a superintendent, but her mentor believed in her capabilities as a leader and verbally promoted her as such. Mary constantly asked herself, "Why would anyone want that job?" But the mentor was adamant in his beliefs about her qualifications for the superintendency.

Mary's role as a high school principal was crucial in her securing the superintendency. A different mentor had told her that if you can run a high school successfully, you could pretty much run a district. The high school principal's position is seen somewhat universally as good training for the superintendency, the mentor stated on more than one occasion. Coming off her year in research at the university and finding herself in need of legitimate employment, Mary applied, hesitantly, for one superintendency. Her paperwork was in order and her references were strong and very supportive. Mary prepared ahead of time for the interview, even driving to the school district the day before to make sure she knew how to get to the interview with plenty of time to spare.

The interview process in this particular school district was divided into four segments—an initial screening interview with the search consultant, who just happened to be one of the influential people to whom her mentor had previously introduced her; a formal interview with all members of the school board; another interview with many school and community constituent groups (faculty, staff, parents, and community members); and finally, an informal dinner with members of the school board. With the exception of ordering pasta with meat sauce for the dinner, which may have had dreadful consequences if she had spilled something on her clothes, Mary felt quite good about how she had presented herself to the school board and all the subsequent community members.

To her delight, Mary was successful on the first try for a superintendency. Her final competition was a male administrator from another district who was seeking his first superintendency also. After working for a short period of time as superintendent in the new district, the school board president shared with Mary why she was the successful candidate for the position. He told Mary that the board members discussed, during the search process, which candidate they would like to be sitting around the table with at midnight some night when there was a problem in the district. The five male school board members unanimously decided that she was the one. It was a match and Mary had successfully attained her first superintendency.

BACKGROUND

Superintendents are the CEOs of the school district. They are responsible for the educational health and welfare of the students in their school district communities. In the everyday workings of a school district, superintendents deal with issues surrounding organizational change, communication, curriculum and instruction, assessment, federal and state mandates, budget and finance, politics, student achievement, personnel issues, strategic planning, school law, and the media (Dadey, Brown, Fensom, Hansen, Kinsella, Quadrini, & Whitehill, 1998; Volp, Archambault, Rogers, Service, Terranova, Whitehill, Brown, & O'Connell, 2001; Volp, Terranova, Service, Fale, Archambault, Brown, O'Connell, & Cattaro, 2004; Williamson & Hudson, 2003). A successful superintendency requires a vast array of personal and professional knowledge, skills, and experiences.

One of the national issues facing school leaders is the equitable hiring of women and persons who represent minority populations for top school leadership positions. Historically, women have been underrepresented in such educational leadership positions as superintendencies. In a historical account by Blount (1999), women held 28 percent of the nation's superintendent positions in 1930. The Association of California School Administrators (1997) reported that the states with the highest percentage of women school superintendents included Delaware (26 percent), Nevada (24 percent), Rhode Island (24 percent), California (23 percent), and Arizona (22 percent). More recently, data indicate that the national average of women superintendents is only 14 percent (Brunner, 2001).

Professional organizations of superintendents have regularly studied their own membership within each state. For example, New York State's professional organization for superintendents is NYSCOSS (New York State Council of School Superintendents). This organization has conducted studies over the last ten years or so, looking at age, gender, salary, working conditions, hot topics facing the superintendents, retirement considerations, and plans for the future. In 2000, there were 18.4 percent of the superintendencies filled by women in New York State, an increase of women school leaders from 8 percent in 1991 (Volp et al., 2001; Volp et al., 2004; Volp, Whitehill, Davis, & Barretta, 1995).

Snapshot V, which is the most recent summary of data collected on the superintendency in New York State, discovered that "women now comprise 22.1 percent of superintendents in New York. The trend is persistent: over the last six years, women have been hired at a steady rate of nearly 30 percent of all vacancies" (Volp et al., 2004, p. 5).

As in many professions, gender is an issue that begs study. Research on women in top educational leadership positions has been ongoing. However, the study of the superintendency has received the most attention. Several studies on female superintendents, focusing on gender differences in leadership styles, indicate that women have a more collaborative approach to leadership than do men (Aburdene & Naisbett, 1992; Bjork & Keedy, 2001; Bjork & Rodgers, 1999; Funk, 1998, 2004; Helgesen, 1990; Logan, 1999; Shakeshaft, 1987; Tallerico & Tingley, 2001; Wesson & Grady, 1995).

In her study of women superintendents from over twenty years ago, Shakeshaft (1987) indicated the following as barriers to women's entrance into and advancement in school leadership: prevalent and overt male administrator attitudes against hiring women, lack of motivation on the part of women to seek administrative positions, and discriminatory practices used in hiring and promoting women administrators.

Barriers for women in the superintendency were found in a national study conducted by Brunner, Grogan, and Prince (2003) for the American Association for School Administrators (AASA). These barriers included bias in the superintendent search process, male-dominated professional networks, and the clash between home and work roles. Additionally, the selection of school superintendents, particularly recruitment practices and the search process itself, has also been studied in individual states (Kinsella, 2004).

AASA conducted another nationwide survey of superintendents in 2006. Topical portions of the survey included career path and preparation, working conditions, contract and evaluation, board-superintendent relationships, and personal demographics. The findings support previous research that the superintendency is a key position in both leading and managing a school district. The survey results indicate that females are less likely than in the past to begin their first superintendency in a small school district. Women appear to be leaving building leadership positions, going to central office directors' jobs, and then on into the superintendency, be it in a large or small district. On the national level, females make up 21.7 percent of the current superintendents, which is comparable to that of New York State (Glass & Franceschini, 2007).

Much more needs to be learned about women who hold educational leadership positions as superintendents. Women recently have gained greater access to the superintendency and are slowly filling the ranks of this top school leadership position (Huynh & Nolan, 2005). Knowing other women's successes and how they achieved the superintendency can make a difference for aspiring women school leaders. Previous research has investigated barriers experienced by women pursuing top school leadership positions and the personal sacrifices these women made for their career success (Gilmour, Kinsella, Moore, Faber, & Silvernail, 2005). Analyzing what has worked and why some women have been successful is the next step.

METHOD AND TECHNIQUES/DATA SOURCES

The objectives for conducting this study center on developing an understanding of women's access to these positions, focusing on what hinders or helps women attain, sustain, and succeed in these key school leadership positions. The study focused on what worked and how successful women attained and retained the superintendency.

Several dozen female superintendents were interviewed in different settings. All but one of the names of the women interviewed have been changed for confidentiality purposes. Within this book, there are several names used as illustrations for characters, which represent a composite of the responses from those superintendents interviewed for this research study. They are not intended to be followed as one would follow a character in a novel, but rather as references for certain experiences of these superintendents. Many superintendents were interviewed in one-on-one, face-to-face situations in their own school district offices. Others were approached at statewide conferences and asked similar questions. Still others were queried in collaborative networking gatherings.

The women superintendents interviewed for this research were eager and willing to share stories of their successes and their failures. These are all portrayed here, highlighted by vignettes, followed by research-related pertinent information, and concluded by important tips for aspiring superintendents of the future.

The setting for this study was in several geographic regions across New York State. Initially, the data were collected in the summer and fall of

2005 through personal, face-to-face interviews with current female school superintendents. The purpose of the study was to focus on what works for these female superintendents. We wanted to know what attitudes, beliefs, practices, and behaviors were perceived as being helpful to these women as they sought to either secure the position of superintendent or retain this position. Data were analyzed and themes emerged.

For all initial subjects selected for study, the interview centered around the following questions:

- Tell me about your career path to the superintendency.
- How many searches were you in prior to obtaining this position?
- What are your experiences in the superintendent search process?
- What made you stand out from the other candidates interviewed?
- What skills, dispositions, and personalities were attributed to the school district hiring you?
- Why was this district a *match* for you?
- What behaviors of the search consultant were utilized to help you move forward in the search process?
- What kind of mentoring, networking, and/or preparation did you experience for the superintendency?
- Would you please talk to me about the process for negotiating your contract?
- What can others learn from your successes?
- Why do you do what you do?

As in many research studies, initial survey questions led to further inquiry. This study was no exception. Follow-up questions for all female superintendents interviewed for this study were asked and answered via e-mail, phone contacts, and additional face-to-face meetings. This next set of questions included:

- How did you prepare for your interviews?
- Did you have any role models and how did they influence you?
- Was the salary portion of your contract settled in the high end, low end, or middle range?
- What have you done to develop a positive relationship with your school board?

- How do you handle criticism from the school board or from the community?
- How have you maneuvered the political waters of your school district?
- How have you successfully worked with the media?
- How have you learned the *business basics* of the job?
- For the application paperwork and subsequent interviews for the superintendency, what have you done to enhance your candidacy for the position?
- Can you offer any tips for aspiring superintendent candidates on paperwork (résumé, references, application, and cover letter) and interview skills?
- Has being a superintendent changed you in any way?
- To whom do you go for counsel or advice?
- While we recognize that each superintendency has its own specific set of circumstances, what observations would you make about who is successful and who is not in this job?

Additional interview sessions with female superintendents were conducted at state-level meetings and in informal professional development circles, thus further contributing to the rich data of the study.

WHERE TO NEXT?

The remainder of the book is organized into several chapters. Chapter 2 describes how the women successfully obtained the superintendency. Their own stories, both of professional success and failure, give the readers a glimpse of what these women encountered along the way and how they dealt with different issues. Chapter 3 suggests strategies engaged in by these female school leaders that helped them stay in their superintendent roles once they had attained the position. Again, personal stories are at the heart of the reading.

At the end of each individual topic in both chapter 2 and chapter 3, a section labeled *In a Nutshell* lays out bulleted information from the section that we deemed critically important. The main ideas are highlighted and segmented out for the reader's attention.

Chapter 4 focuses on the *bigger purpose*, a distinctive look at an emerging body of knowledge supporting leaders' reflective practices, which adds a new context to understanding successful school leadership. *In a Nutshell* also highlights the important points at the end of chapter 4.

Journaling is central to chapter 5, with questions asked and writing space provided for reflection. These questions were designed to guide aspiring school superintendents to create their vision of leadership and perhaps formulate entry plans for future superintendencies. The appendixes include information to enhance the readers' understanding of the journey taken by those interviewed for this book.

The journey of discovery in this research was one of great excitement. Sharing with others what was learned from successful females' quests for the superintendency is the result of the authors' many years of experience as practitioners in the school leadership field, as consultants and researchers in the superintendent search process, and as leaders in the field of training future school administrators for all school leadership positions.

The big question remains: Are *you* ready for the superintendency? We hope so. Read on and enjoy!

2

GETTING THERE

DIFFERENTIATED CAREER PATHS

Sandra was in her second superintendency, having reached this leadership level through the educational ranks from teacher to building principal, central office administration, and then her first superintendency in a small, rural school district. Most of her superintendent colleagues had journeyed professionally in a similar fashion. A few others, one of them being Rosalie, started in the private sector. Rosalie had come from a private construction company, with a career change into education through a classroom door as a teacher.

Rhonda had worked as a teacher's aide while she studied at a local college to be a teacher, which she eventually became before settling into an assistant principal's office and then on up the ladder into the superintendency. Sabrina and Tess had both started their professional careers in the health field, the former as a school psychologist and the latter as a registered nurse. They both realized that school leadership was a worthwhile pursuit and they set out after it.

Sarah and Zoe both took perhaps the least likely road to the superintendency. The first position Sarah held in a school district was as secretary to the superintendent in the school district in which she resided. From this position, Sarah was a key figure in all the happenings of the superintendent's office. She learned by doing and by being in the company of someone from whom she could learn. The knowledge and skills she developed in the course of this job served her well. After many years in that secretarial position and with additional college degrees, training, and state certification, Suzanne was promoted to assistant superintendent for business. Her years of experience as the school business official paid off, as she then became superintendent of schools in a neighboring school district.

Similarly, Zoe began her career in education as secretary to a district superintendent in a Regional Educational Center. He saw in her a potential for school leadership. He suggested to her one day that she should consider returning to college to pursue a career in education. Zoe took his encouragement to heart. She started in schools as a teacher's aide, then classroom teacher, building leader, district-level administrator, and finally into the superintendency. Given the encouragement from a mentor and through her hard work, Zoe reached for the stars and attained the top school leadership position.

Women play many roles and travel many roads in their journey to the top school leadership position in a district. Career paths are varied. There is no one-size-fits-all or one road to follow.

There is *no one way to the top in any school district.* From their initial employment in a school district, many eventual superintendents worked as building leaders and then worked in some capacity in central office administration. Those central office positions included responsibilities in curriculum and instruction, special education, athletics, personnel, business and finance, special programs, grant writing, staff development, directors of elementary and secondary education, reading/literacy, and technology in both school districts (rural, suburban, and urban) and/or regional educational center organizations.

Sandra and most of her superintendent colleagues started their professional careers as teachers (Grogan & Brunner, 2005). This is oftentimes where the real learning, and thereby the career path to the superintendency, begins. This classroom experience, where they learned what really matters in a school district, provided aspiring school leaders with basic skills necessary for most administrative positions. Classrooms have proven to be great training grounds for future school leaders. As Sergiovanni attests, "Teacher leadership is key. Without teacher leadership we can change how things look but not how things work" (2008, p. iv).

Teachers hone both their professional and personal skills each day in the classroom.

- They develop skills in planning and organization, student management, record keeping, filing reports, and communication, both written and verbal.
- They are provided professional development opportunities in instruction, curriculum, and technology.
- They hone their interpersonal skills and relationships between teacher and student, teacher and teacher, teacher and parent, and teacher and administrator.

Additionally, teachers have opportunities to spread their wings and take on potential leadership responsibilities outside their classroom. Building-level and district-level committees are oftentimes comprised of teachers and school leaders, sometimes along with school board members, community residents, business people, students, and parents. The committee work can range from shared decision making to academic booster club to student support team to budget advisory. Superintendent learning happens in each of these settings.

Teachers often step up to take on leadership roles in their union—at the building level, district level, and sometimes on into state and national teachers' organizations. Training in contract negotiation and management fuel some teachers' thirst for school leadership as an administrator. This association in professional organizations provides teachers with many opportunities to cultivate knowledge and skills for the superintendency, as well as add to a developing professional network of mentoring and support.

College and university advanced-degree programs leading to a state certification in school administration further the learning and experiences of qualified teachers. Coursework is designed to meet the needs of those aspiring to be building leaders, district-level leaders, and/or school business officials. The classes in these programs of study present the students with opportunities to learn from others, to discover and formulate their personal beliefs about education and its leadership, to network with other students located throughout the region, and to put theory into practice through a supervised administrative internship portion of the program.

Students in these advanced-degree program classes interact with others who aspire to be school leaders and thereby set the early groundwork for important networking systems. As will be discussed later in the book, in the world of the superintendency, it is more often about whom you know than what you know.

Teachers who eventually become state certified as school leaders oftentimes move into building principals' positions. While some superintendents start their administrative career as assistant principals, some go directly to the principal's office and others skip this step altogether. Through the coursework of their advanced-degree programs, school leaders have had their eyes opened wide to the machinations of the school building and district. In the principals' roles, they see this in action. Principals must see the bigger picture. They are responsible for the world beyond the classroom and must meet and deal with all the sometimes conflicting agendas and issues for those whom they lead.

Principals take what they have learned and done at the building level and sometimes move into district-level positions. There is more variety and certainly more responsibility in assistant superintendents' and directors' positions, with an emphasis on the district as a whole. These school leaders may network more in professional organizations. There are mentoring possibilities for fledgling school leaders and, hopefully, many district-level leaders will *pay it forward* in helping others succeed.

At the district level, assistant superintendents and program and grant directors experience more direct exposure to state and federal mandates, with an emphasis on formulating a plan of action to make something work. Women, whose expertise lies in curriculum, instruction, and assessment, oftentimes succeed in attaining the superintendency.

From the platform of district office leadership, many superintendents are born. Superintendents take what they have learned in the classroom, building, and central offices and put all of that to good use. They may lead either individual school districts and/or regional educational centers. They are able to articulate a shared vision for the school district, drawing on their own beliefs, experiences, and needs of the district they are chosen to lead. Superintendents love kids and learning. They come to understand the culture of the schools and the community. They forge ahead to leave a positive mark through their leadership.

Now in her second superintendency, Sandra has learned many lessons, sometimes the hard way, through all her experiences. The career paths of superintendents:

- are varied, with no one sure way to the top
- sometimes begin in a classroom, but not always
- sometimes are planned, but sometimes develop over time and with opportunity
- are carved out over a period of time, so as to develop both personal and professional skills and abilities necessary for the job
- are sometimes nurtured by one or more mentors
- are often supported by a network of colleagues focusing on leadership
- provide a vehicle for a fulfilling professional life

IN A NUTSHELL

- There is not a set professional pathway to the superintendency, but rather many use their successful classroom teaching experiences as a solid foundation for school leadership.
- Teachers who are looking to eventually lead a school district take on responsibilities outside their classroom. Sometimes those leadership roles are in the teachers' union organizations.
- State certification for school leaders occurs through advanced-degree programs of study at colleges, universities, and some alternate pathways.
- Building-level administrative positions are oftentimes good starting places on the road to the superintendency.
- From the building level, future superintendents often move through district-level/central office leadership positions before the superintendency.
- Mentors and networking are often key elements in the career path to the superintendency.

THE MATCH

Olivia and Patricia both did their homework on the school districts in which they were interested in the superintendency. Patricia researched a district that had a residency requirement for the superintendent, so she asked herself if she could live there forever. Even before the interview process began, she traveled to the school district. She ate at local restaurants and talked to people with whom she came in contact. If she was the successful candidate for the job, Patricia would be moving her family there, and she needed to be sure that this would work for all of them. She liked what she saw, and it felt *right*. After a lengthy interview process, the school board offered her the position and the match was made.

On the other hand, Olivia was interested in a school district where there was no residency requirement. To meet her professional needs, she wanted a district that had a reputation as a progressive, rural community, but she did not want to uproot her family in a move away from their home base. She had to take into account her husband's employment and the needs of her two high school–aged daughters. Besides, the whole family was happy where they lived, and Olivia could commute to the job. When the job came, she accepted the job offer. Everyone's needs were met and the match was complete.

Some female superintendents are not married but are divorced, widowed, or single. For these candidates, residency may not be an issue if their support system is composed of friends. However, residency might be an issue, especially if privacy of one's life is at stake. The residency requirement may well be the number one issue in determining the match between person and place.

Olivia and Patricia, longtime friends, were curious. What were the experiences of other female superintendents in determining a match? At the annual statewide conference for superintendents, Olivia and Patricia talked to their female counterparts.

When queried, Nicole related that she was the first person in her family to attempt and succeed at a college education. Her family was composed of blue-collar, hardworking people who were committed to their work. She had married young, right out of high school, but she knew what she wanted and how to get it. With young children at home, she knew that education was a route she wanted to take, and it had proven to be the right choice for her. When it came time in her career to seek the superintendency, the match between the person and this poor, rural school district was there. Nicole was not a stranger to poverty. She held home and basic human values dear to her heart, and those values were reflected in ones held dearly by the school district community in which she sought the superintendency. The fit of person to district and vice versa was achieved.

Another colleague, Paula, was ready for her first superintendency. She had come up through the ranks in education and had three building principalships under her belt. She was a lifelong resident in the county and wanted to remain there. When a position opened that suited her, she checked out the other district leaders who would be her colleagues if she were the successful candidate. What she found suited her professional needs.

Paula had many strengths, but her knowledge and skills to make the match were lacking in the business end of the job. If she were to be successful in her first superintendency (and she wanted to be), then she needed some help in this area. As superintendent, Paula knew that she would be looked upon to be a leader in all aspects of the position. Her learning needed to grow in the business and financial areas of a school district. In this district to which she applied for the superintendency, a strong school business official was currently employed. This person could help her grow and add tools to her already capable professional self. A school leadership position already filled with personnel who would complement her skills and experiences was just what Paula was seeking. This was going to work.

Other superintendents, Yvonne and Sabrina, sought top school leadership positions in school districts that were progressive in nature. Neither one of them could settle for the status quo. Their professional lives to this point had been challenging and forward moving and they would not stagnate. They sought and found leadership roles in organizations that had a track record of progressiveness, with a strong relationship with surrounding school districts. Yvonne and Sabrina believed in and exercised a collaborative approach to leadership in their respective school districts, which helped seal the deal for their fit with their districts.

As they sought more information on the match or fit of a person with the superintendency and vice versa, Olivia and Patricia stumbled upon this issue of superintendents' community involvement. Interestingly, in her first search for a superintendency, Wanda found no match. The first district's expectations were that the new leader would ally him/herself with community groups, such as the Elks Club, and church groups. This was not what Wanda was comfortable doing. On her second try, she found a needy district that warranted assistance she could willingly and skillfully provide. She was confident that this one was a match and said, "I can help."

Sometimes, school districts seek new leaders who are unlike the superintendent who is leaving. Vivian had school-aged children, and the community saw her as a parent with whom they could identify. She followed a top-down leader whom she had disagreed with when she worked as his assistant superintendent. The community was ready for a female leader who would work for both girls and boys in the district, as opposed to Vivian's predecessor, who the community thought focused on boys only. They liked her people skills and her skills as a communicator. Vivian's personal attributes fit the district.

Ruby, like Vivian, followed an embattled male in the superintendent's position. She was hired after a highly publicized criminal case involving this male superintendent and sexual improprieties with a female teacher in another district. The district was badly bruised from all the negative press surrounding the former superintendent, and Ruby, as an out-of-district candidate, was seen as someone totally removed from the situation. The district wanted to get out from under the negativity and get back to the student learning tasks at hand. As a leader in the school district, Ruby has overcome the baggage left from the former superintendent and is moving the district back into a position of strength in the county.

Olivia and Patricia took note when they heard this next story. Both Roberta and Stella affirmed that physical appearance, in their experiences, played a part in the selection of a superintendent. While there is no hard and fast data to support this phenomenon, Roberta and Stella strongly believe that when they first interviewed for a superintendency, the fact that they were younger, thinner, and more attractive opened the door more readily for them in the interview process. Was this part of the match and/or fit of the person to district and vice versa? It sounds disappointing, but possibly true.

Olivia and Patricia's heads were spinning. So what can be discerned from the experiences of all these women? How does the *match* happen between a school district and a successful superintendent candidate? What lessons can be learned from all these women?

The match, or fit, of a school district to superintendent is as crucial as that of the reverse—the superintendent to the school district. The person, the institution, and its community must gel for a successful relationship to be possible. The match works both ways, with both professional and personal issues at the center. If it does not, the relationship often sours and both the person and the school district seek relief in the form of a new, more workable situation.

To get a better handle on the match before accepting the position, a candidate for a superintendent's position should consider *doing a district scan to garner vital information.* This can happen via the Internet at the state education department website and/or the individual school district's website, through local publications, and via professional networks, to name just a few avenues. Additionally, preparing an entry plan is just one way that some superintendent candidates solidify their beliefs and expertise in leadership, thereby checking for a school district–person match.

The *human connection is key to the relationship* between superintendent and those whom she leads. "It's not about the courses you took, your finance background, or the doctorate you have. It's the human connection," related school board member, Audrey Cullinan, when she was asked about the candidates the school district had just interviewed in their superintendent search process (Kinsella, 2004, p. 291). Candidates' credentials and associated paperwork provide the necessary confirmation of certification regulations, educational levels, experience, and any other professional requirements the district sets in establishing its profile for a new superintendent. However, liking the person is what gets the candidate the job. The *who* factor rises to the top in the superintendent selection process (Vail, 1999).

What qualities school districts look for in a superintendent vary from place to place and lead to the match. Successful superintendents' personal qualities of being clear, honest, direct, straightforward, responsible, collaborative, accountable, open, easy, relaxed, trustworthy and trusting, credible, passionate, committed, outgoing, confident, upbeat, authentic, diplomatic, and a lifelong learner are attractive to school boards and the school community as a whole.

How does an applicant from out of state ensure that match? At the very least, potential out-of-state candidates for a superintendency should gather important district information off the school district's website. As was previously mentioned, networking with other school leaders familiar with the area is critical for success. Search consultants stress that potential candidates from out of state must make a compelling case for themselves that they have knowledge, skills, and experience in specific statewide learning standards and assessments for learning. If not, they will be at a disadvantage and may not make it into the candidate pool for a specific position. A definite plus for any applicant for the superintendency is the accolades earned from successes in leadership and student achievement as leaders of school districts in other states.

The match or fit between person and school district and school district and person is of the utmost importance for the successful professional relationships of all involved (Williamson & Hudson, 2003). The job of the superintendent is far too crucial and difficult for the person and/or school district people to not be happy. At best, it is a tough job that takes special talents and abilities. The match is critical to a successful superintendency.

IN A NUTSHELL

- It is critical that there be a match between person and school district and vice versa for all those seeking the superintendency.
- Reasons behind the match between superintendent candidates and school districts vary as much as the candidates themselves.
- The overall quality of life in a school district oftentimes is one of the key deciding factors in the match of the superintendent to the district.
- Sometimes the search for a professional and personal fit between school district and its leader takes time and patience.
- Along with the personal attributes a candidate may bring to the search process, professional considerations also weigh heavily in

the decision-making process when selecting a new school super-intendent.

- Persons from out of state may experience difficulty in the application process, but should do what is necessary to be considered a viable candidate.
- Physical appearance may play a part in the selection of the superintendent.
- Serious applicants should seek school district information via the Internet, through local publications, and/or through a professional network.

THE RIGHT PAPERWORK

Nancy saw a superintendent opening in a particular school district, and right away, she was intrigued. She was ready for a change professionally and this might just be it. She had numerous years of experience in school leadership and felt that she just might be the right candidate for the position. In order to be a viable candidate, she needed to first traverse the application process. How would she ensure she had all the right paperwork?

Nancy worked on her résumé. She made a habit of updating her résumé frequently, making sure that she clearly addressed all the leadership experiences she had had, with supporting data that was current and accurate. She stressed that she must be herself, in both the way she presented herself on paper and in person. Nancy made sure that all her paperwork was perfect—no typos, high-quality paper, organized, and thorough, with her experiences written in such a way that they reflected what she would do as a superintendent rather than merely a recap of previous roles, responsibilities, and accomplishments. She included her e-mail address so that communication regarding the position could happen through many avenues.

As a regular practice in preparing for a job search, Nancy contacted the search consultant, looking for an understanding of what the school district and board of education valued. She then crafted her application materials to reflect what she had discovered. Nancy believed in doing all the homework necessary to be as complete an applicant for the position as she could be. She left no stone unturned.

Nancy realized that there are three parts to the application process, in addition to the formal application itself. The cover letter, résumé, and reference list must be professional, up-to-date, and specific to the position to which she was applying.

In the cover letter, Nancy knew that she must grab the reviewer at the outset. Doing homework on the school district in which the employment opportunity existed was a critical piece of preparing to write the letter. She did this by reviewing the school district's website, gathering information on the district off the state education department website, reading local newspapers, and seeking district-produced public relations documents (e.g., newsletters and websites). The background information Nancy discovered helped her craft a more direct and personalized cover letter.

Nancy portrayed concrete examples of her leadership accomplishments in a very succinct manner. She matched her accomplishments to what the school district specifically needed, as was delineated in the superintendent vacancy brochure. She used the cover letter to reveal herself to the school district decision makers for the superintendency in which she was interested.

Nancy also knew that there were two other parts to the application paperwork—résumé and list of references. The résumé must be an honest portrayal of the candidate. Nancy knew that others, though not necessarily those looking for a superintendency, had fabricated their education, work experiences, honors, and/or other qualifications when they applied for jobs. This fabrication, when discovered, led to public humiliation, rebuke, and oftentimes loss of a coveted professional position. Nancy did not want to be in that group of unsuccessful people.

As she continued to prepare the paperwork for the superintendency application, Nancy looked for opportunities that stretched her professionally and added to her already ample toolbox of leadership knowledge and skills so that these might enrich the quality of her résumé. To continually prepare herself for the superintendency, Nancy participated in professional development activities from a nearby state university.

The Superintendent Development Program (SDP) at Oswego State University had a reputation for building and enhancing school leaders' skills through a series of cohort-driven activities, taught by current, successful superintendents from around New York State (Gilmour & Silky, 2002). In addition to simulating situations that superintendents might face in the course of the job, the SDP also provided networking opportunities for all involved. Nancy cultivated her leadership skills and a support network for future use. She wanted to be portrayed as a lifelong learner. She believed that all superintendents must model this practice.

Nancy's references were updated all the time. She used personal and professional references that would benefit her candidacy for the super-intendency. She made sure that all her references knew beforehand that she was applying for a certain position and that they agreed to support her bid for the top job. Selecting quality people as references is a critical step in the application process. In this business, Nancy knew that it is *who* you know that oftentimes gets you noticed. Key people in profes-sional and personal circles can open doors for those on the way to the superintendency.

Additionally, Nancy asked her colleagues what they did to get their foot in the door. Her friend, Stella, had a mentor, who was also a dis-trict superintendent of a Regional Educational Center. He had served in the capacity of a search consultant for several school districts in the vicinity, and he willingly reviewed all Stella's application materials be-fore she sent them out to a school district. This extra pair of eyes served as a check for the correctness and appropriateness of her application. If Stella makes it past the application status to candidate status in her search for a school superintendency, she makes it a practice to prepare a folder, personalized for the specific school district, for each member of the school board with whom she will be interviewing. These are distrib-uted before she begins the actual interview. On one side of the folder is Stella's résumé. On the other side, she includes documents that relate who she is and what she has done. She includes a data piece, with sup-porting information and documentation showing her decision making. Stella also crafts a three-year entry plan that she shares with the school board. Stella is thorough in promoting herself with quality paperwork, representing herself in the highest professional manner.

Nancy took all of this good practice under consideration when apply-ing for the job she wanted. What had she learned? Had she followed all the proper steps in preparing the paperwork for the application process? Would her carefully crafted paperwork get her in the door as a candidate for this superintendency?

The cover letter, professional résumé, and list of references are vitally important to one's candidacy for the superintendency. While the match or the fit of person to district and district to person oftentimes seals the deal in securing a superintendency, *proper paperwork is one critical part of opening the door for the interview process itself* (Noe, Clark, & Colwell, 2006). If you don't get in the door to interview, you will never get a superintendency.

Candidates should be prepared to complete at least part of the application process online. While this is not always the case, *more and more school districts are requiring applicants to submit materials electronically*. Computer skills, for obvious reasons, are key to a person's successful search for the superintendency.

Honesty is a must when portraying one's personal and professional life on a cover letter and/or résumé. Lying or fabrication of accomplishments, educational background, awards, and/or experience is unacceptable and has led to some people losing jobs they worked a lifetime to achieve.

In applying for a superintendency, there are several right ways and wrong ways to construct a cover letter (Minicozzi, 2007). They include, but are not limited, to the following.

1. What your cover letter looks like is as important as what it says about you. Be neat and care about how the letter makes you look.
2. Address the cover letter to the specific person who will be doing the reviewing of the application materials. Do your homework. "Dear sir or madam" will not suffice.
3. Be specific to the particular job opening when writing the cover letter. Match your own experiences and skills to those mentioned as being needed by the school district in question.
4. End the letter in a strong manner, speaking to how you will follow up on the submission of the application materials.
5. Limit your statements in the cover letter to one page only. Your writing should be succinct and to the point.

6. Check the spelling of all proper names in addition to the rest of the information in the cover letter.
7. Be specific as to what skills, knowledge, and abilities you will bring to the school district as its new leader.

People listed as references should be knowledgeable of the applicant and supportive of one's candidacy for the superintendency. They should also be contacted before being used as a reference to make sure they are willing to speak positively on your behalf. Candidates should know if the reference could talk about you for your next step in the search process. Also, know if the reference can write a compelling letter on your behalf. If there is any question as to whether or not a reference will speak *for* you in a superintendent search, then do not use that reference. Ask someone else whom you are certain will help you.

Potential candidates for the superintendency should check directly on the websites of the state education department, state superintendents' organization, or state school boards' association for *exact names of those people who may be part of the actual interview* groups. By using correct names in any form of communication, an astute interviewee looks sharp and may gain positive ground in the search process.

Finally, those candidates for the position, no matter what the outcome, should consider *sending a follow-up thank-you note*, individually addressed, to each member of the school district with whom they interviewed. Again, this simple gesture may be the edge that makes a world of difference in a school district's search for a superintendent.

IN A NUTSHELL

- The right paperwork in a superintendent search includes a cover letter, a professional résumé, and a list of references, in addition to any application form a district may require.
- The application materials may have to be submitted in an online format, so applicants should hone their computer skills.
- All paperwork should be authentic and an honest representation of who the applicant is.

- People used as references should have firsthand knowledge of the applicant's leadership qualities that are essential to the superintendency.
- Proper paperwork gets the applicant in the door from applicant to candidate status.
- Pay attention to the right and wrong way to submit application materials.
- Address all written communication to the appropriate person, using that person's correct name and title, if applicable.
- A thank-you note, sincerely written, may follow an interview and should be addressed to specific people.

THE SEARCH PROCESS

There were all kinds of stories. Women had a variety of experiences, whether it was their first try for a superintendent's job or embarking on a search for a subsequent school superintendency. They talked about a number of issues. Tina, a first time superintendent, related that she attained the superintendency by being in the right place at the right time. As an assistant superintendent for curriculum and instruction, she moved into the interim superintendent's position when her direct supervisor, the superintendent, was seriously injured in a car accident. When he chose not to return to the position but rather to retire from the district, Tina declined the school board's request that she apply formally for the superintendent's position. The school board had decided to do a national search for a new superintendent.

Despite Tina's refusal to enter the candidate pool for the position, the school board, after some discussion, approached her and offered her the superintendency without a search process. Timing in life is everything. The injured superintendent was able to retire and take care of his health. Tina was able to move into a position she did not actively seek at this point in her professional career, and the district was able to maintain continuity by hiring someone who already was in the district and had a proven track record of competence.

Tina sought others' insight. Some women had successfully attained the superintendency each time they had tried. Others went through the process multiple times and were eventually successful. There were differing experiences with those women who had been internal candidates for the superintendent's position. Tina had been a successful internal candidate. A few others experienced rejection in their current district but, after searching outside that district, were welcomed into the position in a new district. Unfortunately, some still were not successful despite repeated attempts, and it was not until much later that they were able to secure a superintendency. A few others became frustrated after repeated attempts to attain a superintendency. These women chose to stop seeking the top job and remain in their current school leadership positions.

The process of searching for a superintendency often includes many elements that candidates do not expect. One common strand, as Teresa came to understand, included a heavy dose of interview time with school board members. Candidates spend formal time interviewing with the school board, plus are informally interviewed at dinner or other social situations with the school board. Other stakeholder groups—teachers, students, parents, district administrators, community members—are also part of the process, most often as segments of group interview sessions throughout a daylong process in the school district.

Teresa had long heard about the glass ceiling for women leaders and the active "good-old-boys" network, but she was unsure if both existed. Several of her contemporaries cautioned her that the good-old-boys network was still in existence in the search process for some superintendencies. Teresa had run into the system in the form of the male search consultant, a Regional Educational Center district superintendent hired by the district's school board to guide them in their journey to find a new school superintendent. The successful candidate felt the consultant could have done a better job when it came to brokering her contract. She felt the Regional Educational Center district superintendent gave her no options for a higher salary. "Take it or leave it" was his bottom line to her.

Does this ultimatum happen to all candidates? Would this happen to male candidates as well as female? Teresa is still bitter about this experience and is working closely with the current Regional Educational Center district superintendent (a female) to advance her cause financially in her continuing contract. She is finding this current working relationship far more collegial and supportive.

A different colleague, Stella, felt there was gender bias as she searched for a superintendency. In her first attempt at securing the superintendency, the district hired a white, older male, someone whose profile the school board found matched that of his predecessor and with whom the school board was more comfortable, instead of her. On her second try, Stella was successful. She found her own fit with a district where three school board members, the decision makers, were women. She was home.

Successful superintendents experience a match between the board and their style and values. The balance of men and women on school boards varies greatly, and if women on the board adhere to the *queen-bee syndrome*, there may be some reluctance on their part to hire a female. The thinking of the queen bee is that I got where I am on my own (school board member) and you need to get your position on your own. Thankfully, Stella had not experienced this.

Female representation on school boards can have a positive or negative impact on the female candidate. You just never know for sure, as can be attested by the stories related so far. Regardless of the gender balance on a school board, those boards that have not had an opportunity to discuss or embrace the idea of a diverse candidate pool can severely limit the possibility of attaining a position for candidates who differ from a traditional model. In this model, successful candidates are still white males (Volp et al., 2004).

And yet, a third colleague of Tina's felt there was age bias in her first attempt at securing the superintendency. Granted, Sabrina was younger than some of the other candidates for the position and clearly younger than the retiring district superintendent for whom the replacement was sought, but she was an internal candidate, a known quantity, and had a solid pedigree and proven leadership knowledge and skills. Sabrina was eventually passed over for the position and later found out that hers was just a *courtesy* interview given to someone in the number two leadership position, as the assistant superintendent.

Today, she remains somewhat miffed about the whole experience. The school board hired an external candidate—an older, white male, who, once again, was in the image of the retiring superintendent. But, not to worry, Sabrina landed a different top job on her second try and, to hear her tell it, has never been happier.

Whew! Tina was exhausted from all the stories, and she had much to ponder. What did it all mean? How could she sort it out so that it made sense? What had she learned? Her move into the superintendency had not been similar to her colleagues. She was tapped, supported by a board that knew she would be successful, and moved into the position without some hurdles experienced by others.

Consultants are integral parts of the search process. Whether they are privately hired or the school board turns to the Regional Educational Center district superintendent for assistance, search consultants are gatekeepers for people and information. While search consultants do not legally have the authority to hire a superintendent, they are in a position of power in the process. Search consultants wield influence in allowing some candidates to move forward in the process, from applicant to candidate status. By using their professional and personal network, search consultants recruit applicants for the superintendency (Kinsella, 2000). If there is to be equity in the field, search consultants need to consciously promote women and persons of color as they assist a school district in hiring a new superintendent.

Some consultants have been known to keep a stable of superintendent candidates, shifting them from one search to another. For example, candidates who complete paperwork, have a screening interview with the search consultant, or interview with the board and stakeholder groups and are not successful in one search, may automatically be considered during the consultant's next search. Historically, search consultants have long been a controlling factor in a school district's search for a superintendent (Moody, 1983).

There is a great deal of ethical debate about keeping such a stable, and many search firms will not engage in this practice. Candidates who choose to work with these firms need to resubmit their paperwork for each search. The paperwork needs to be detailed and specific to each district that the candidate is interested in serving as the superintendent.

Although there is an attempt not to keep a stable, search consultants do network with one another and are aware of who is looking, who might be tapped, and what qualifications might best fit a particular district. It is important for the candidate to be seen as being selective about where he or she applies and not just throwing her or his name into every available search.

Confidentiality in the search process is sometimes breached (Kinsella, 2000; Kinsella, 2004). Tina became aware of a colleague's seventeen-day journey from start to finish through an entire superintendent search process. Ursula had attained her first superintendency in this short a time frame. The search consultant had promised her complete confidentiality in the process and had come through for her. Ursula, like many applicants for the position, was an assistant superintendent in a different district and wanted to keep the search as quiet as possible. She was not looking to burn bridges in the district in which she was currently employed, but was actively seeking to leave.

This is not the typical scenario in the superintendent search process. The superintendent of schools is a very high-profile, public position and finding a new one generates much community attention. School district stakeholders, such as teachers, students, staff, parents, business people, and senior citizens, are often participants in the search process. Candidates' names get leaked, and their personal lives can come under great scrutiny in the community (Kinsella, 2000; Kinsella, 2004). Candidates for the superintendency should realize that their professional and personal lives might become public fodder in the school district rumor mill.

It is also important to know at what point in the search to withdraw if the position is not a match for the candidate. Those who wait until they are offered the position to decline, do themselves a disservice for future searches. It is a small business and those who falsely lead on a consultant or board are often viewed as engaging in unethical behavior. Once the first screening interview has taken place, the candidate will have knowledge about the district and its issues. Certainly, after the first interview with the board, the candidate should be aware if there is a match. Withdrawing from the search at either of these points is understandable. Waiting until the position has been offered is not generally acceptable professional behavior unless there is a problem with coming to agreement about a contract (Kinsella, 2000; Kinsella, 2004).

The attorney for one district, for example, convinced the board that they should include a clause in the superintendent contract that specified that the superintendent would have no due-process rights should the board decide to terminate his or her contract. The first candidate who was offered the position subsequently declined the job. So did the second. The third person was not a strong choice of the board, but was the only one who was left. Although they were able to get rid of him quickly due to this clause, they endured leadership that was not congruent with their goals or values. This school board will be careful not to have this clause again so they can attract the best possible candidates.

Some women in their search for the superintendency experienced *gender and age bias*, being perceived as too young or too old. Many women do not seek their first superintendency until after they have raised families (Grogan & Brunner, 2005). They may be seeking their first position in their mid-forties or early fifties. Consultants again play a critical role in the bias game. Some consultants work hard to bring before a school board female and ethnically diverse candidates. However, school districts sometimes look to replace one leader with someone with the same image. School districts know and are familiar with one *type* of school leader and are unable and/or unwilling to step outside that comfort zone. Women are gaining access to the superintendency, but gender and age bias still are present in some searches.

For example, after several years in her superintendency, Sally learned that the search consultant was instrumental in breaking through the stereotypes the board held against hiring a woman. During the initial meeting with this board, at which the profile for the position was being developed, the all-male board specifically told the consultant that they did not want to hire *one of those*. Not quite clear what *one of those* meant, the consultant kept calm, and every time the board members said, "He must be able to do x," she casually repeated their comment as soon as she could as, "He or she must be able to do x."

At first, the board members were taken aback, but then started to correct each other when they referred to their future superintendent as only a male. It became almost a contest for each member to correct the others, and although at first it had a mocking tone, the barrier was broken. Ultimately, they hired the best candidate for the position; it was Sally.

When Sally heard this story after five very successful years as superintendent in this district, she was totally surprised. During the past five
years, each board member had taken a turn being the board president
and they had all been remarkably supportive of her and her initiatives.
They had voted to extend her contract and were very pleased with her
performance. They were able to go beyond their previous notions of
what a successful superintendent should be like, and they embraced the
best possible candidate for their district. This is a win-win situation.

While the school board is ultimately responsible for hiring the superintendent of schools, other parties or stakeholder groups are very
much a part of the search process. In addition to school board members,
candidates for the superintendency can expect to interview in some
manner with parents, students, teachers, district administrators, and
community members. This is oftentimes in both formal and informal
settings. School boards hire superintendents, but stakeholder groups
provide input on the superintendent candidates in the decision-making
process. Stakeholder groups are often part of the community rumor mill
regarding some candidates' personal and professional qualifications,
which has been known to stymie a search or two (Kinsella, 2000). The
degree of input and school community involvement varies from district
to district.

There are many models for the search process, and some districts engage in confidential searches in which only board members are involved.
Ursula's experience in a superintendent search took only seventeen days
from first interview to signed contract. The search consultant, a female
district superintendent of a Regional Educational Center, and school
board members kept the process completely confidential. That is hard
to do, but, in this instance, it worked for all the parties involved.

What might the search process look like? Here is one example of possible steps in a process in which the board elects to involve stakeholder
groups:

1. The board determines if they will invite possible search consultants to talk with them about being hired to conduct the search. If
   so, search consultants are invited in to present their proposal for
   the search. The board then selects a consultant to complete the
   search.

2. The search consultant meets with the board to determine the timeline for the search, advertised salary, residency requirement, and advanced-degree requirements. Consultants also check to see if there is an internal candidate. If the internal candidate is being seriously considered, does the board need to engage in a full search or possibly just develop the profile to determine if this individual matches what the board is looking for in a superintendent? If the internal candidate will not be considered for the position, the consultants work with the board to determine who will speak with this individual who will ultimately have to work with the newly hired superintendent or will need to leave the district.

3. The search consultant and school board members meet again to develop the profile—what do they want the superintendent to know, do, and be like? The consultant meets with a variety of stakeholder groups independently to hear their thoughts regarding what they think the future superintendent should know, do, and be like as well as answering the following questions: What are the hallmarks of the district? What does each group perceive to be the biggest challenges that the new superintendent will need to face in the next five years? Teachers, support staff, students, administrators, district office staff, parents, and community members all provide suggestions, which are then passed along to the board for their consideration. It is important to remember that regardless of the input from the stakeholder groups, who will be hired is the school board's ultimate decision.

4. After reviewing the data from each group, the board clusters responses, looks for commonalities and themes, and creates the final candidate profile.

5. This profile, along with demographic data from the district and the application process are included in a brochure, which is widely distributed within the state or on a national level depending upon the board's preference to engage in a national search. A variety of advertising avenues are considered.

6. Consultants review all applications and résumés as these arrive, and then they set up screening interviews for each individual who appears to match the profile developed by the board. Interviews may be held in person or over the phone or webcam, depending

upon the distance involved. Candidates might also engage in interviews with search consultants at local, state, and national conferences where career or search centers and services are provided.

7. Once these interviews are completed, the consultants prioritize the top ten candidates; however, they bring the paperwork from everyone who applied to a meeting with the board so the board has access to all paperwork. The consultants work with the board to reduce the number of candidates from ten to six. All names and information are confidential at this point.

8. Consultants work with the board and stakeholder groups to develop a series of questions that they will ask each candidate. The consultants also provide a workshop to help those who will be interviewing clarify legal and illegal questions.

9. Each of the six successful candidates is invited to interview with the board. This is a one-hour interview with only the board. Following the interviews the board will cull the list to the top three candidates whom they wish to invite back for full-day interviews.

10. Board members and stakeholder groups are now all aware of the names of the three finalists. Their paperwork is kept in the district office for all to review. Board members begin their own reference checking, knowing that stakeholder groups may also be doing their own checking.

11. Each candidate comes to the district for a full day to meet with each stakeholder group, tour the district, tour the community to gain information regarding available real estate should they need to move to the district, meet with a designated spokesperson for the district (typically, an administrator or the current interim superintendent), and finally, meet with the board for dinner and an informal meeting.

12. At the end of each stakeholder meeting, the group completes a reporting form for the board. These reports are passed along to the board after the interview with each candidate.

13. After the third candidate has completed his or her interview, a representative from each stakeholder group will be invited to briefly present the findings from that group to the board.

14. The board will then use this data as well as their own to make its decision. The successful candidate will be contacted, and based on the desire of the board, there may be a site visit by the board to the candidate's current district.

15. Once the candidate has said yes, the contract is negotiated with the assistance of the school district's attorney and the candidate's attorney or assistance from professional organizations such as American Association of School Administrators (AASA) and/or an affiliate.

16. If no candidate can be agreed upon or the contract negotiations fall apart, the board may choose to offer the position to their second choice, begin the search again, or hire an interim superintendent and engage in a search at a later date.

Another model that is similar to the one described above looks like the following illustration. Steps that are different from the previously described model are noted with an asterisk (*):

1. The board determines if they will invite possible search consultants to talk with them about being hired to conduct the search. If so, search consultants are invited in to present their proposal for the search. The board then selects a consultant to complete the search.

2. The search consultant meets with the board to determine the timeline for the search, advertised salary, residency requirement, and advanced-degree requirements. Consultants also check to see if there is an internal candidate. If the internal candidate is being seriously considered, does the board need to engage in a full search or possibly just develop the profile to determine if this individual matches what the board is looking for in a superintendent? If the internal candidate will not be considered for the position, the consultants work with the board to determine who will speak with this individual who will ultimately have to work with the newly hired superintendent or will need to leave the district.

3. (*) The search consultant and school board members meet again to develop the profile—what do they want the superintendent to know, do, and be like? Unlike the above search, the consultant

does *not* meet with a variety of stakeholder groups prior to the board developing the profile. The consultant will meet later to see if there are other suggestions that the board might like to consider.

4. Consultants review all applications and résumés as these arrive, and then they set up screening interviews for each individual who appears to match the profile developed by the board. Interviews may be held in person or over the phone or webcam, depending upon the distance involved. Candidates might also engage in interviews with search consultants at local, state, and national conferences where career or search centers or services are provided.

5. Once these interviews are completed, the consultants prioritize the top ten candidates; however, they bring the paperwork from everyone who applied to a meeting with the board so the board has access to all paperwork. The consultants work with the board to reduce the number of candidates from ten to six. All names and information are confidential at this point.

6. Consultants work with the board and stakeholder groups to develop a series of questions that they will ask each candidate. The consultants also provide a workshop to help those who will be interviewing clarify legal and illegal questions.

7. (°) Each of the six successful candidates is invited to interview with the board. This is a one-hour interview with only the board. Following the interviews the board will cull the list to the top three candidates whom they wish to invite back for full-day *mixed-stakeholder group* interviews.

8. Board members and stakeholder groups now are all aware of the names of the three finalists. Their paperwork is kept in the district office for all to review. Board members begin their own reference checking, knowing that stakeholder groups may also be doing their own checking.

9. (°) Each candidate comes to the district for a full day to meet with a mixed group of stakeholder members. The stakeholders are divided into half. The candidate will meet with each group. Another candidate might be interviewing with the opposite group. Following or preceding these interviews there is an informal cof-

fee hour at which anyone is welcome to talk with the candidate. Finally, the candidate will meet with the board for dinner and an informal meeting.

10. (*) At the end of each mixed stakeholder meeting, the group completes a reporting form for the board. These reports are passed along to the board after the interview with each candidate.

11. (*) After the third candidate has completed his or her interview, a representative from the stakeholder groups will be invited to briefly present the findings from that group to the board.

12. (*) The board will then use this data as well as their own to make its decision. The successful candidate will be contacted, and based on the desire of the board, there may be a site visit by the board to the candidate's current district. The board may choose to visit the districts of all three candidates in this model.

13. (*) Once the candidate has said yes, the contract is negotiated with the assistance of the school district's attorney and the candidate's attorney or assistance from professional organizations such as American Association of School Administrators (AASA) and/or an affiliate, such as the New York State Council of School Superintendents (NYSCOSS). The search consultant will also help with contract negotiations in this model.

14. If no candidate can be agreed upon or the contract negotiations fall apart, the board may choose to offer the position to their second choice, begin the search again, or hire an interim superintendent and engage in a search at a later date.

Many variables come into play to determine which option is the best for the district. Regardless, it is important that the board unanimously support the candidate who is being offered the position. If the search fails and the district chooses to engage in a search immediately, the school board will need to change one or more variables significantly or they will get a weaker candidate pool than they had the first time. Generally, this means either increasing the salary or letting go of the residency requirement.

Knowing the steps in the search process in advance can be a great help to candidates. Those candidates who ask seasoned superintendents or search consultants to review their paperwork and conduct mock interviews are better prepared and may be more confident during the process.

Finally, as Tina learned in her case, *being an internal candidate is sometimes beneficial to your candidacy for the superintendency, but as seen with her colleagues, sometimes it is not.* Candidates need to know that sometimes districts offer interviews to internal candidates only because they are already there, hence the "courtesy" label. Armed with that information beforehand can help a potential candidate decide whether to look elsewhere when seeking a top job in a school district (Grogan & Brunner, 2005). Hopefully, someone in the district has taken the time to talk with the internal candidate to avoid bad feelings and resentment. This is especially helpful when the internal candidate who is not being seriously considered for the position will need to demonstrate professionalism and work with the new superintendent or will need to leave.

IN A NUTSHELL

- Search consultants, whether they are Regional Educational Center district superintendents, university professors, or from a private firm, are the gatekeepers of the superintendent search and selection process.
- The search process in any school district may take on one of several formats. Candidates for the superintendency should be clear about the expectations in the process.
- Gender and age bias may be factors in a school district's decision to hire a new school leader. Have a plan or examples of what you have done to surmount any areas in which these barriers may be present.
- School boards, while oftentimes considering the input of other parties or stakeholder groups, are ultimately responsible for hiring the superintendent of schools.
- Internal candidates experience mixed results in successfully attaining the superintendency.

BARRIERS TO OBTAINING THE POSITION

Sandra openly admits that gender was a barrier to the superintendency for her. Some of her predecessors in the profession had broken through this barrier, so she viewed attaining the superintendency as possible, not impossible. The task was not insurmountable. She did encounter certain individuals who deemed her gender as a negative for her candidacy for the position. However, there were three female school board members in the district to which she applied. This helped, not hindered as in a "queen bee" situation, her successful attempt at securing the position.

Patricia, in the first superintendent search in which she was involved, felt that she was the token female candidate brought by the search consultant before the school board and community. There was no proof of this, just a gut feeling. Patricia was working in one of the area school districts prior to applying for the position, so there was some history between her candidacy and the school district she wanted to lead. She did get the job, but feels that her father being a former superintendent was a major influence in the school board's decision to hire her.

Many successful female superintendents had positive experiences in the superintendent search process. Teresa, Wanda, and Paula were approached by their male district superintendents and recruited to apply for the superintendents' positions they now hold. Many of their colleagues in the superintendent ranks consider the district superintendents and other superintendents, both male and female, to be mentors who have supported them in any number of ways. Some mentoring assistance came in the form of conducting mock interviews for the candidates, while others helped candidates phrase responses to questions in a particularly strong way. Barriers for one can oftentimes be helpful to another.

School boards can sometimes, but not always, be a barrier to a woman's search for the superintendency. For example, in Patricia's second search, the school board of the new district was still reeling from a front-page sexual scandal involving the recently resigned former superintendent. The new school board, in an attempt to learn all that there was to know about Patricia, visited her current district and probed deeply into her professional and personal life.

The school board in Patricia's current district felt their counterparts in the new school district, who conducted an inquiry into many private matters, had assaulted them. Patricia was a bit singed by the process also and looks back at it now as a tough lesson learned. The process undertaken by the new school board was intrusive and complete. They were protecting their interests and did not want to get burned again.

Teresa was a strong external candidate for the superintendent's position. She was a familiar entity in the organization and thought she stood on good ground in the hiring process. But the school board, ultimately, decided on another candidate, one who more closely matched the retiring superintendent. Teresa was from a rural area, and this was a city school district. Her rural background made the school board members less comfortable with her candidacy. She was disappointed with being passed over but went on to secure a different school superintendency shortly thereafter.

Rhonda believes that her connection with influential people in the surrounding areas of the school district that had the superintendency opening allowed her to have an easier time navigating any barriers that may have existed in the search process. She had previously cultivated the support of a district superintendent of a Regional Educational Center, as well as other superintendents in the area. She used these connections to help her secure the superintendency and avoid any barriers.

Nancy stresses that the fit is essential. If candidates experience barriers, then they need to keep trying and secure a superintendency elsewhere. There are enough school districts out there with varying clientele and needs for almost anyone to find a fit.

Do barriers exist in this day and age of conventional wisdom? What does experience and research tell us? What do future female superintendent applicants need to know to break through any barriers that they may encounter?

Gender has long been a deciding factor in who gets what job, but not all experience this phenomenon (Williamson & Hudson, 2003). This is particularly true in male-dominated positions, of which the school superintendency is one. Gilmour et al. (2005) found that many female superintendents acknowledged no gender barriers existed in their attaining the superintendency. These mixed results and allegations of a good-old-boys network are just as confusing as those of the queen bee syndrome, where women are kept at bay by other women who believe that they got where they are on their own and others should, too. Gender is a factor, but it could work in your favor also.

The embarrassing transgressions of a former superintendent may provide a barrier for those seeking to follow in that position. This can be true for both women and men. Candidates for the superintendency may undergo far more personal and professional scrutiny, as school boards are often smarting from the public sting of a superintendent gone wrong.

The issue of privacy in one's personal life may be a barrier to which some applicants for the superintendency do not want to reveal themselves. Nadia, as aspiring superintendent, shared her sexual orientation with a search consultant and district superintendent. Although she is a highly qualified assistant superintendent, she has not been moved forward on any searches since she disclosed this information. She now fears this is a mistake that cannot be undone.

School boards are sometimes in the habit of hiring in a like mode. They are comfortable with what they know and have no intention of hiring a superintendent outside that comfort zone. In a historically male-dominated profession as the school superintendency, this is a major barrier with which candidates must deal (Vail, 1999). Hopefully, search consultants work to guide a school board through a decision-making process that includes both women and people of color as viable candidates for the superintendency.

"It's whom you know, not what you know" is a saying that is applicable to the superintendent search process. Applicants with connections more often become successful candidates for superintendencies than those who are unknown. The human connection is a powerful influence in the decision-making process. Outsiders may experience this as a real barrier to getting in the door of the superintendency.

While the issue of a match, or fit, between person and district and vice versa has been discussed previously in this chapter, it needs to be addressed here also as a potential barrier for some candidates for the superintendency. *The match between person and district is a key issue*, and it is a positive if the fit is there, and clearly a negative if it is not. Applicants should not despair if one or more attempts at attaining the superintendency fail. The fit is key, and if it does not exist, then applicants should keep trying in other districts, searching for that one that will be a fit for both person and school district.

IN A NUTSHELL

- There are mixed indications of gender as a barrier to attaining the superintendency.
- The queen bee syndrome can be just as much a barrier as the good-old-boys network.
- Past negative transgressions by former superintendents may provide barriers for those seeking to immediately follow a disgraced superintendent.
- Applicants for the superintendency should realize that sometimes personal privacy and confidentiality in the search process are breached.
- School boards may have a mind-set as to whom they will hire as a superintendent, keeping in mind someone with a likeness to the superintendent leaving the position.
- Most barriers to the superintendency can be neutralized by strong, positive human connections to powerful and influential people.
- If the fit between person and district and district and person is obvious, barriers can be overcome.

MENTORING

In chapter 1 Mary talked about the key role her mentor played in encouraging her to become a superintendent. He had tapped her for this role. Marcia, on the other hand, sought a mentor to assist her in obtaining a superintendency.

Marcia thought she was doing all the right things to find a mentor. She was networking with her local superintendents (Gardiner, Enomoto, & Grogan, 2000). She was conducting informational interviews with district superintendents of intermediate units across the state. On numerous occasions she attended professional development opportunities and women-in-leadership meetings to connect with other leaders around key instructional issues. She was on several listservs for future positions and received openings posted by search consultants. She met with a variety of search consultants and heeded their advice. She e-mailed contacts that superintendents recommended. She read voraciously about the job to enhance her conversations with possible mentors. She completed district scans to have concrete data to share. She actively searched for a mentor (Daresh, 2001).

Then, Marcia made a series of mistakes. In hindsight, they may actually have been insightful gifts. She entered her first mentoring relationship because of her mentor's charisma. He was well liked and friendly and introduced her to all the right people. He chose her to mentor from all the others in her cohort group. He invited her to dinner with other veteran superintendents and offered to have her co-present at a state conference.

But when she took a closer look, he really didn't share the same passion for instructional issues that she did. In talking with him, he minimized the importance of these issues and challenged her to only focus on the business, political, and public relations sides of the job. Marcia knew these elements were critical to her success, but she wanted to blend all aspects of the position together. His joking manner, though intended to be playful, ended up being hurtful and embarrassing. He dismissed her as being too stodgy and told her to get a thicker skin.

Next, she chose a female superintendent because the woman had achieved what Marcia hoped to achieve, a superintendency in a challenging but doable district. At their first meeting, this potential mentor was very encouraging and supportive. However, as Marcia attempted to call her over the next several months, she repeatedly got her voice mail and her e-mails were unreturned. When they finally did connect, the interchanges were once again warm and helpful. Marcia contacted her again after this meeting and the same pattern of no response developed. Though the potential mentor was well meaning, she just didn't prioritize the time to connect.

Marcia became much more weary about seeking or being chosen by another mentor. She decided to accept the encouragement to engage in a mentoring relationship with a veteran superintendent who had taken her under her wing in the past and had helped her obtain her current position. This mentor was very supportive of Marcia now becoming a superintendent; she took Marcia with her to conferences, meetings, and dinners and spent many hours helping her hone her paperwork for the search process.

As Marcia gained confidence, she began to attend some of these same meetings by herself or with other professional colleagues. Her mentor perceived her as ungrateful and ignored her. Marcia tried to talk with her mentor but was rebuffed. She thought this behavior seemed similar to the behavior of teenagers, not professional women, and became very disappointed at the way the relationship ended.

Marcia stepped back. What had she learned from these three attempts? First and foremost, she learned to engage in a mentoring relationship with a mentor who *has similar values* and, although some priorities might be different, has similar goals. The mentor must also possess *the skills, knowledge, and dispositions* that the protégé needs to make achieving these goals possible. Ethical behavior is a must and cannot be compromised to gain access into the right circles or to be the center of attention in professional circles.

Second, however well meaning the person is, a true mentor *makes time* for this relationship. Choosing or being chosen by a very capable mentor is essential, but the protégé must determine the stage of this person in his or her own professional career. If the focus for the mentor is filled with other initiatives, the mentoring relationship might better be that of a role model than a true mentor. A true mentoring relationship requires ongoing access and connection with the mentor, knowing that *ongoing* may be defined very differently depending on the individuals involved.

Third, the nature of a mentoring relationship is that it is *hierarchical*. The mentor is in the position of power based upon knowledge, access, position, and so on. Often it is the mentor who begins the relationship and the protégé who, once he or she gains confidence, knowledge, and skills, unconsciously or consciously tries to transition the relationship from a hierarchical one to one as equal colleagues. If the mentor isn't ready to let go, the relationship can end with the mentor having feelings of ingratitude and hurt. Engaging in a dialogue along the way about the mentoring relationship and what the needs are for both individuals helps to provide a healthier and smoother transition to a new collegial relationship.

As we move from seeking mentors to being mentors, which could happen simultaneously with different individuals, remembering the pitfalls and ingredients for successful relationships is essential.

A Bit about Mentors—Where Do I Find One?

Both female and male mentors are identified. Mentors are identified from earlier positions in the careers of superintendents as well as from more current positions. These mentors were principals, superintendents, and intermediate unit district superintendents. Annabelle, Jane, and others talked about their mentors also being from outside education. They were husbands, partners, mothers, and spiritual leaders and reflected a variety of other roles.

Gilmour (1983) noted in her research twenty-five years ago that mentors who came from these roles could be very helpful in supporting the courage and self-reflection necessary for leadership roles. Remembering that the mentor often initiates the relationship and the protégé seeks to transform it to a different, more equal level, this may cause problems if the mentor is a family member, spouse, or partner.

Mentors come from the field, from a wide range of positions. Mentors may also emerge from formal mentoring/professional development programs such as the Superintendent Development Program (Gilmour, Kinsella, & Silky, 2003). Faculty members for this program are current superintendents who design specific sessions on many topics for these aspiring superintendents. A similar program described by Kamler (2006) in her research on the superintendency included topics such as the following: understanding the superintendent's role; attainment of knowledge and skills; networking and fellowship; reflections; and support and encouragement. Superintendent mentors also noted benefits including intellectualism, collegiality, and legacy.

Informal mentoring programs or opportunities both personal and professional were also noted. Although not always identified as a mentor, *outgoing superintendents in the district* where individuals are assuming the superintendency provide helpful information for the transition.

Betty talked about mentoring behaviors that include providing support for accessing the superintendency and thriving once in the position. Mentors and protégés discuss career consulting regarding the following: what positions to take; those to avoid; how to choose a particular position; encouragement to move to another position; and specific skill mentoring in areas such as budgeting, athletics, negotiating, legal issues, boardsmanship, and addressing political aspects of the superintendency.

Annabelle and others commented that their mentors said to remember to *ask for help*, and it is acceptable to call for assistance. Advice from mentors include the following: listen, listen, listen; don't do anything for the first six months you take the job; it's okay to ask for help; practice answering questions like a superintendent would answer them, not as you would in your current position (principal, assistant superintendent).

Mentoring may be *short or long term*, but it must be ongoing within whatever timeframe is agreed upon by the mentor and protégé. Janet, who was dealing with her first capital project during her second week on the job, needed help. She contacted her current mentors and they put her in touch with some specific resource people in financial advising and construction management who became her mentors through the project. She has called on them three more times during her five years in the superintendency. Although she doesn't need to connect with them a great deal during times when she is not engaged in a project, she knows just who to call and get the help she needs.

Mentors who know when to call are so valuable for beginning superintendents. Eleanor commented that her mentor almost had a sixth sense about calling. Just when she was heading into turbulent waters or a report for the state education department was due, he would call just to check in with her. She is now a veteran superintendent and provides the same mentoring for other superintendents. Eleanor believes that "we all want each other to succeed. There might be competition during the actual search process, but once we're in the job, we are a strong network of support for one another."

Mentoring that helps the individual learn not only *the skills needed* for immediate survival in the position, but also the ability to become a more *reflective* administrator and instructional leader is key. We also know that mentoring is particularly helpful to women and underrepresented groups. There is still a dearth of successful superintendents who represent these groups. It is difficult for women and persons of color to not only gain access to the superintendency, but also gain experiences in the positions that are looked upon most favorably by school boards when hiring their superintendent.

Superintendent Betty commented, "I had a hard time convincing the board that my background in elementary education would serve me well as their superintendent. One board member commented that he wasn't sure I could handle all the important decisions that take place at the high school level." She went on to say that she had not been successful convincing her superintendent in her previous district to allow her to move to the high school when she was an elementary principal and the high school position became available. A colleague of hers in a neighboring district did just that so she'd be more marketable to those board members who still believe that being a high school principal is the stepping stone to the superintendency.

Frances related that a mentor truly taught her to have the courage to lead. Her female mentor also recommended that Frances have a diverse group of mentors and not just females. She suggested that one should find mentors who have the experience and power to open doors. Make sure they are diverse in position, gender, race, and perspectives.

Kathleen suggests the following advice that she has learned along the way. One specific mentor of hers was a search consultant. The consultant urged her to get an evaluation from someone who hires or recruits superintendents. All sorts of people who hold the appropriate certifications believe that they are ready to take that leap into a superintendent search. Kathleen knows because she was one of them. But because of the unusual path that she was taking in trying to get there, Kathleen knew that she needed help in ensuring that she had filled the gaps.

So, she made an appointment with a couple of people who led professional searches for superintendents on behalf of boards of education. Who better to be candid with her? These connections were made by her superintendent and through her own personal contacts with former superintendents.

Were they candid. She went to these individuals well before she knew that she would be ready to apply so as to give herself time to appropriately and honestly fill any gaps. Kathleen went to them again after she believed that she had put in enough time and effort to be well on her way and received a second review. She went a final time when she believed that she had done all that she could to make herself a viable candidate.

This process was successful on a couple of different levels. First and foremost, Kathleen is certain that they would have told her to not waste her time if they really thought that her goal was a bit too lofty with the credentials and background that she had. If that were the case, Kathleen would not have submitted applications in vain and wondered why hers never got out of the paper pile.

Equally important was that Kathleen was making herself known to people who could recommend her as a solid candidate. She had established a professional and purposeful relationship. After all, she sought them in a mini-consultant role, followed their advice, and grew from the experience. If Kathleen were to try for another search, even though she has the experience of being a superintendent, she would still get a recheck. The field has changed and she would still need to know if she had gaps yet to fill.

Superintendents suggested that aspiring superintendents find two mentors, one in the field of education and one outside the field of education. Kathleen had the good fortune over her entire career of having mentors and coaches usually in an informal manner. When she was working on attaining her building- and district-leader certifications, she had the privilege of working directly with her superintendent as her mentor. She also had a business leader in the community who had retired from successfully running his own business as her other mentor.

This was exceptionally helpful to have both an expert and successful person in the field of education as well as one from the outside. When she would discuss a project or problem, she had the benefit of experience and someone else questioning why or should situations be handled in a particular way. Kathleen was always thinking both inside and outside the box, so to speak. As we know, the mechanics of education can be very foreign to someone who did not have to deal with unions, civil service, politics, and so on. To have to tease through the details really helped her think through decisions or pathways to decisions.

For Kathleen both of her mentors were male. The key piece is not gender but the knowledge, skills, and dispositions you need to tap at various points in your process of attaining and retaining the position of superintendent.

Mentors make a critical difference in candidates being able to obtain their first superintendencies and in helping new superintendents maintain their positions and thrive. They assist with getting there and staying there in the role as superintendent.

IN A NUTSHELL

- Engage in a mentoring relationship with a mentor who has similar values.
- Select a mentor who possesses the skills, knowledge, and dispositions that you need for achieving your goals.
- Find a mentor who makes time for this relationship.
- Find multiple mentors for diverse purposes.
- Remember, the nature of the relationship is hierarchical. Is your mentor ready to let go when you are ready to become more independent?
- Be careful of first impressions. Potential mentors might be charismatic and initially welcoming but have little follow-through.

Where do I find a mentor? First, who might these individuals be in your current setting? Next, look for the following:

- That part within yourself that is willing to be vulnerable, will actively seek a mentor or mentors, and will ask for help
- Both female and male mentors from diverse backgrounds
- Those who assume diverse roles within the field
- Formal mentoring programs such as the Superintendent Development Program
- Those who come from informal mentoring programs—personal and professional
- Retiring superintendent in the district who may serve as a helpful mentor
- Those who respond and will take the time when you ask for help

- Professional networks (see Networking section of this chapter)
- Opportunities to engage in short- or long-term mentoring sessions around specific topics or skills in your current setting, such as a capital project, budget preparation, or dealing with the media
- Those who have vision and are reflective
- Those who possess and model the courage to lead in inclusive settings that are equitable for all

NETWORKING

Why Networking?

Diane had a mentor who supported her when she was dealing with a board member who was looking out for his own children at the expense of other children. She was trying to pull together a budget that would pass this year since last year's was defeated. Additionally, she was revising a mission statement that was ten years old, and she was still trying to find enough family time while balancing all the demands of the job.

What she missed was a network of like-minded and like-positioned individuals from whom she could gain multiple perspectives on issues. She needed to find just the right person to help with the capital project or to share some humorous moments and frustrations that needed to remain confidential.

Not only was mentoring a critical factor for success for Diane and many of the female superintendents to whom you have been briefly introduced, but networking was very beneficial for them also. Lack of professional networks was one of the major barriers for women accessing the superintendency (Czubaj, 2003) Also related to this was a lack of welcome in the "old-boys" network and a lack of influential sponsors. Juanita knew this to be true for Latina candidates, and she found networks such as OALA (Oregon Association of Latino Administrators, www.btp.pdx .edu/OALA.php). Frances agreed this was true for African American aspirants. These obstacles seem to be true for both men and women from diverse groups (Méndez-Morse, 2004). Developing diverse connections with experienced leaders at the local, state, and national level is very helpful when attaining and retaining the position of superintendent.

Keys to Effective Networking

The key to networking is *the net*. The job of superintendent is so immense that to consider taking on one more task seems impossible. Yet, many of these women had strong networks and had taken the initiative to cast out their net—to create, join, and lead networks that supported them professionally and personally.

Juanita and Betty commented on two keys to networking that were echoed by many others. One was establishing them and the other was maintaining them. Superintendents seemed to flow in and out of what they needed from their networks. If they were working on a capital project, those contacts were essential, but then they were let slide as they moved on to other priorities. If the connection was firmly established, the players would be there the next time their expertise was needed. There seemed to be a shared sense that we are all in this together and need to help one another.

The American Association for School Administrators (AASA) sponsors a women's conference each fall in the Washington, D.C., area. Those who attend are able to network with career and search consultants as well as men and women who help to provide skill enhancement in areas such as negotiations and marketing. Each year the conference is posted on the AASA website at www.aasa.org.

When conducting superintendent searches, one of the attributes that boards are looking for is visibility. They are looking for this visibility within the district and within the community. This visibility can be a true asset for superintendents. Frances notes that belonging to local civic organizations can help one make valuable connections when seeking external funding for district initiatives, developing skills such as public speaking and website enhancement, and garnering support for future budgets. Annabelle joined the local Lions Club, becoming an ambassador for the district, and was able to obtain financial support for a technology initiative.

The networking doesn't always have to be professional. Linda talked about joining a yoga class. She knew if it was on her schedule she would attend. If it was left up to her to go when she wanted to, she always found a reason why she was too busy. That's why going to the gym never worked for her. At the yoga class, Linda was able to network with an editor of a local newspaper, a woman starting her own small business, and a grand-mother who had a history of the district and the neighborhood to share. Linda was gaining necessary exercise and time to breathe while creating a network of support and sharing that was fulfilling.

Some states have women's organizations to help promote women in leadership. The New York State Association for Women in Administration (www.NYSAWA.org) promotes gender-balanced leadership and advances equity and diversity in schools. Local affiliates offer periodic programs and social gatherings for leaders at all levels. A statewide conference is held each year featuring statewide, national, and international presenters.

Interesting here, however, is also the belief for some that belonging to an all-female organization for networking can hurt rather than help. Beth, Joanne, Barbara, and Monique talked about not wanting to be stigmatized by joining such an organization because their male counterparts looked down on it. Bell and Chase (1996) found that although women knew that women could be very helpful in their pursuit of the superintendency and could offer specific mentoring tips, they were careful about belonging because of what male colleagues would say.

Although Juanita and Frances participate in activities of an all-female networking organization, they are very careful to remain active in organizations and networking structures that go beyond primarily single-gender or single-race membership. They do not want to minimize their access to the superintendency. They want access based upon their potential and talents, not their gender or race. Gardiner et al. (2000) found that women and persons of color seek to keep "themselves from succumbing to the attitudes and beliefs that discriminate against so many others like them" (p. 189).

At a statewide superintendents' conference, Juanita and Frances were talking with their female and male colleagues of color. Of the 700-plus school districts within the state, only 20 were led by persons of color. This approximate 3 percent was not aligned with the diversity in the student populations within the districts statewide. It was also not aligned with the national average of 6 percent (Glass & Franceschini, 2007). They were brainstorming how to increase the number of candidates for the superintendency and focused on the opportunities that lead up to strong candidacy for individuals regardless of race or gender.

How do they help students of color gain access to better learning and more leadership roles so they can in turn become leaders at all levels within the educational ladder? How are we supporting teacher leaders of color? What about those at the middle level of administration? And let's not forget those ready to take the step into the superintendency.

Not only did these superintendents know that they needed to belong to networks, they also felt the need to lead them once they had their feet on the ground. They accomplished this by presenting at national conferences to expand their networks.

Now that online resources are so accessible, there can be virtual networks as well. Forty-nine states have a superintendents' organization that provides ongoing support and networking for superintendents. The AASA Affiliated Associations Executive Directors Roster may be found in appendix C at the end of this book.

The National Association for Female Executives (NAFE) provides leadership opportunities and networking opportunities for women (www.nafe.com). Women at Work Network is also one for enhancing networking beyond the school environment, with information about this organization available at www.womenatworknetwork.com. These networks are suggested because they encourage superintendents and emerging superintendents to take their educational agenda to a broader audience; if we truly are going to change our schools, community support is essential. Belonging to these broader networks provides opportunities to become involved in the businesses in our communities and to meet some of the movers and shakers who may someday comprise boards of education. Important information can be gathered at www .winconference.net/Become_a_speaker.asp.

IN A NUTSHELL

- Remember there are two keys to networks: establishing them and maintaining them.
- Seek opportunities that might include the following:
  - Women's conferences, such as that sponsored by AASA
  - State Women's organizations, such as NYSAWA

- ◦ Civic connections
- ◦ Networks that combine personal growth with professional affiliations such as yoga classes; book clubs; or religious, spiritual, or social justice groups.
- Remember to keep networks broad and not all single gender, single race, or single purpose.
- Don't wait for the networks to find you. Take the initiative to discover existing networks or create ones that are needed.
- Publicize these networks for others to join either formally or informally.
- Be a role model for the type of networker you believe to be trustworthy, ethical, and available.
- Remember national and international conference opportunities for networking, attending, and presenting.
- Try to have networks for multiple purposes and in multiple modalities including the following:
  - ◦ Face-to-face
  - ◦ Electronic: e-mail, blogs, Skype
  - ◦ Small group related to specific topics
  - ◦ Small group for emotional support
  - ◦ Extended networks for specific skills or visioning.

SUPERINTENDENT CONTRACT NEGOTIATIONS

In talking with the female superintendents, several stories about not negotiating contracts to their maximum advantage came to light. Allison and her colleague Jeff completed a superintendent preparation program at the same time. Several members of their cohort group attained positions. Allison and Jeff were offered positions in adjacent districts. There was a salary range for each position. Jeff requested the highest limit of the salary range stating that he was the candidate they wanted and, as such, he should be paid the highest salary. Allison believed that since this was her first superintendency she should take a mid-range salary. In hindsight, she realizes that she could have driven a harder bargain during her initial negotiations and requested a higher salary. She did know

there often was a double standard for men and women during the negotiating process and men still seemed to have more bargaining power.
However, the question might be asked, "Do men have more bargaining
power, or do they just negotiate better? Do they take time to find out
what the district can support financially?"

Several women stated they did not want to appear greedy, so they
took a lower salary, while citing their males counterparts were much
more firm about their salary demands. Linda not only took a salary at
the lower end of what was advertised, she also compromised on her
compensation package. She did not consult an attorney during this process and wished that she had. Contacting an attorney, your mentor, or
a superintendent organization is essential during these initial contract
negotiations. Many organizations will offer this as a free service to new
superintendents.

Most initial packages are standard. However, some superintendents
earn up to 50 percent of their salary in additional perks such as the following:

- car allowance or mileage reimbursement
- holidays
- vacation time
- moving expenses or residency expenses—if you say you will move
  into the district, this commitment needs to be honored. (With the
  shrinking candidate pool, more and more districts are going to
  residency preferred.)
- additional health insurance
- disability insurance—(Annabelle was able to turn her disability insurance into salary and was able to buy back unused vacation days
  at a per diem rate, which added nicely to her salary.)
- annuities
- professional development funds
- memberships in professional organizations
- merit pay, which is becoming increasingly common for those superintendents who reach certain goals
- longevity, which may be something to negotiate if you plan to stay
  in the district a long time
- contributions to a TSA

- date of determination—the date by which the school board will formally set your salary for the upcoming school year. (Many districts set this at a time that is away from the pressure of budget votes if one is taken by your district.)
- other expenses: cell phone, home computer, PDA, fax

Diane talked about working with search consultants who reinforce with the board that they must be ready to pay the top end of their advertised salary. They must work with their community to realize that it often takes more money to replace the outgoing superintendent. This didn't sit well with Diane's board, but they were able to work through an agreement that allowed for a greater percentage in her second year once she had proven herself.

Maria told us that *for every move there is a countermove.* She took their initial offer and gave a counteroffer for salary and some elements of the compensation package. She was careful in doing so lest she appear to be more interested in the money than in serving the district. She tried to anticipate and prepare for the reactions of the board and knew that her listening skills would be very helpful. What were they saying about her value relative to the package being presented to her? She knew she needed to decide her bottom line and then move toward closure of the negotiations.

Betty knew *there was both a rational and emotional side to negotiations.* Just as Maria talked about her listening skills, Betty believed that really hearing the board went beyond the rational package put on the table. She knew the outcome would be a combination of both. She tried to engage in a collaborative negotiations process so that both she and the board would feel they had been heard and had greater value than before they began this negotiations process.

Three different styles of negotiations seemed to emerge. Most of the women engaged in what we might call *soft* negotiations. They more or less took what was offered. Frances and Eleanor took more of a *hard* sell, and they felt they paid for it. While each board had offered a salary range, they were each offered the lower end and did not accept it. Interestingly, they were both preceded by men in their districts who told each of them respectively that they had negotiated their salaries at the top end of the range. One male board member told Eleanor it wasn't ladylike to be so aggressive. This board member would continue to give her a hard time until she moved on to a different district.

A third type seemed to be more of a *collaborative* process in which the new superintendents could talk about how their compensation packages reflected the quality of performance they intended for the district to best meet the needs of students. Bringing as much as possible back to the students was effective in creating a working relationship at this initial stage with the board.

Current research on salary ranges for superintendents was reviewed. Many factors must be taken into account when interpreting these figures, but they provide a general guideline for what is currently being offered.

Glass and Franceschini (2007) found that nearly 47 percent of superintendents had a three-year contract, while 25 percent had a four-year contract. Some states limit the number of years that a first-time superintendent may be offered or may limit those for out-of-state candidates. Some states allow for *rollover*, or *evergreen* contracts in which there is an automatic annual rollover so the superintendent always has a three-year contract. Only 6.7 percent were performance-based contracts. This rose to 12.3 percent for superintendents in large, urban districts.

If a district wants to include a *No-Fault Termination clause* in a superintendent's contract, it is recommended that the superintendent walk away. Although the district may have to pay the salary if the superintendent's contract is terminated, they do not have to pay benefits, and the superintendent will not accrue time toward retirement. This will also be an issue when the superintendent seeks further employment.

The termination agreement of a superintendent's contract may look like one of the following:

- By superintendent on notice—sixty to ninety days if you accept a position in another district
- By mutual agreement—most contracts
- For cause, with binding or advisory arbitration or by the board

There are so many nuances to the contract that it is advisable to have an attorney who is familiar with these issues involved in your negotiations.

The national mean average for superintendents' salary in 2003–2004 was $125,609; in 2005–2006 it was $134,436. These figures did not

Table 2.1. Superintendent Salaries Compared to Per-Pupil Expenditure

Per-Pupil Expenditure	$9,000+	$8,000–$8,999	$7,000–$7,999	$6,000–$6,999	Less than $6,000
Superintendent Salary	$132,589	$118,657	$123,551	$126,635	$122,895

include fringe benefits. These compensation packages might include any or all of the following: car allowance, membership in professional organizations, health care, worker's comp, term life insurance, and annuities. Over 63 percent of the superintendents were satisfied with their packages. Boards hoped that these packages might help them attract and retain good superintendents (Glass and Franceschini, 2007).

Solomon (2006) found that the average salary in 2005–2006 for superintendents in large urban districts was $187,924; medium urban districts was $161,784; suburban districts was $155,876; small town districts was $112,968; and rural school districts was $91,606.

Education Research Service (2006) looked at superintendent salaries relative to per-pupil expenditure and found the data shown in table 2.1.

Overall, superintendents were satisfied with their salaries. Glass and Franceschini (2007) found that 19.6 percent were very satisfied; 63.3 percent were satisfied; 13.7 percent were unsatisfied; and 3.5 percent were very unsatisfied. There was no significant difference between the satisfaction ratings among men and women. States collect information regarding salaries, but some do not collect information regarding overall compensation packages.

The best way to begin this process is with your mentor and your network. They can provide insights and suggestions from their years of experience, their own successes, and even their own shortcomings in this process.

IN A NUTSHELL

• Do your homework. What are your colleagues making in your geographic region? What do state and national organizations cite as salaries and compensation packages for those with your experience and size district?

- Negotiations are just that. Don't just accept what is offered because you are leery of the process.
- Know your bottom line.
- Get advice or assistance from an attorney, your mentor, and/or a professional organization.
- For every move, there is a countermove.
- Seek a collaborative process.
- There is a rational and emotional side to negotiations. The end result will be a combination of the two.
- For those sitting superintendents, keep checking periodically about how your behavior is matching board expectations and begin conversations about your upcoming contract.
- Think creatively about turning insurance or sick days into salary after your negotiations.

③

STAYING THERE

DESIGNING AND LEADING YOUR VISION AND ENTRY PLAN

Rhonda powerfully proclaimed that, as superintendent, she is the "Keeper of the Dreams." With that as the focal point in her professional life, she drew on her own beliefs in formulating her vision for the district. Education is the answer to success in life, and Rhonda does not waiver from that single statement in her leadership style. It is what drives her each day.

Rhonda has a passion for what she does as a superintendent. To hear her tell it, the passion is very emotional, almost spiritual, in nature. She loves what she does and works tirelessly for children. It almost takes her breath away.

A vision is only as good as those who own and support it. Rhonda firmly believes in community involvement in the development of the vision and in putting that vision into practice. She communicates frequently with her constituency, keeping them informed and moving all of them in the same direction she envisions for the district. Communication works both ways in that as Rhonda actively communicates her ideals, she equally actively listens to the needs and wants of the school community. Blending her beliefs with those of the community is a win-win for all the students in her charge.

Rhonda's school board is a critical component in the realization of her vision for the district. In addition to the regularly scheduled semi-monthly, public school board meetings, she organizes periodic board retreats scattered throughout the school year. At these retreats, Rhonda, two assistant superintendents, and the school board members meet privately and usually away from the school district. Topics of discussion have varied from school finance to instructional updates to visioning for the next school year. By working collaboratively with the school board and school community, Rhonda reaps rewards when children learn in the best possible ways. Keeping the focus on children and their learning is essential.

Rhonda's visibility within the school buildings, at district events, and in the community at large is another method of leading her vision. "I am everywhere," she proclaims. In this way, she keeps a pulse on the district and actively promotes what she believes will positively impact the lives of all school district children.

Rhonda's practice at developing and leading her vision teaches us several things. First, a superintendent's own *personal beliefs on education form the basis for a vision for the school district* (s)he leads (Sergiovanni, 2008; Williamson & Hudson, 2003). Those personal beliefs are cultivated over time. They may reflect the person's own experiences as a young child, student in school, educational professional, and family member. In an AASA (2006) publication titled "Leadership for Change," the 2005 state winners of the National Superintendent of the Year Program suggested several leadership tips. One of the top ten tips stated that superintendents "employ a laser-like focus on the district's strategic plan and do not get sidetracked" (p. 12). The vision may shift and bend in certain situations, but the basic tenets remain firm and strong.

Upon these basic tenets, a superintendent's vision is blended with those needs of the school district. A superintendent, as the leader of the school district, is responsible for molding and communicating the vision and working diligently to move the school community in one direction. A *leader's passion and emotion* help drive home these school community ideals.

Plain and simple, the *key to any superintendent's vision is the children* of the school district (Williamson & Hudson, 2003). The children are the reasons schools exist and school leaders lead. There is a movement forward to make the world a better place for children. A superintendent's legacy should be to leave the district's students with more and better learning opportunities than when his or her tenure in the superintendency began. This is a great gift.

A superintendent's job is 24/7/365. The superintendent is the spokesperson and front-runner in leading the school district's vision. Being accountable to the public is part of that leadership function. Attendance at and participation in community activities and events are essential. The superintendent is always "on the job" (Hammond, 2006). The reward for a job well done is the success of all the district's children.

The term *Keeper of the Dreams* has been used in this section of the book. It means that a superintendent must consistently focus on the question, "Is this good for children?" If the answer is yes, then the superintendent's vision and that of the school district remain on course.

The Keeper of the Dreams Gets Organized

Eileen knew that to be the *keeper of her dreams* she must set about doing so in a very clear manner. Fortunately, organization was one of her strengths, but as she talked she suggested the following elements to an organizational scheme:

- At home: What was needed to make the week run smoothly for her family, including food preparation, errands, chauffeuring, caring for and arranging care for her children and elderly parents, and her own attire?
- In her office: What should be in place for working with her office staff, dealing with chain of command for daily and emergency situations, accessibility, and financial oversight? How had problems been addressed in the past and how would she address them?
- Within the district: How would she get to know all of the stakeholders? How would she especially develop an administrative team and set her responsibilities?

- With the board of education: How would she establish a working relationship and boundaries as well as set board communication and agenda procedures?
- With members of the community: How would she meet with key members of the community, be available to all members of the community, and establish communication mechanisms that were sustainable and effective?

Eileen noted that this list was not sequential. Each aspect carried a great deal of importance, but her first priority should be clarifying her procedures with the board.

Being a Keeper of the Dreams and Developing an Entry Plan

Betty and Frances remember being eager to get started in their new positions. They both adhered to the wisdom of their mentors and developed entry plans that they shared with the board on an ongoing basis. Their plans had similar aspects but were tailored to meet district needs, board priorities, and their individual strengths. Aspects of Betty's and Frances's plans included the following:

- General goals for the board of education, the district, and the community
- What would occur the first day, the first week, the first month, the first six months and the first year
- How these activities would be evaluated to see if they met the proposed goals
- How these goals would be modified and refined with more complete data and feedback

From getting organized to getting involved, these successful superintendents paid attention to detail. They ensured the board received monthly reports such as the Year-to-Date Summary of Receipts and Expenditure Report, the Investment Report, Warrant of Expenditures Print-Out, and the Treasurer's Report. They knew the quarterly reports should include cash flow projections, budget detail expenditure report print-out, school lunch financial report, extra-classroom activity fund, and federal project expenditures reports. These reports may differ from state to state, but it is essential for superintendents to know what is expected and to always be on time or earlier with such reports.

Lily remembered when she was a principal she had a monthly folder of all the memos, flyers, deadlines, and events that she needed to plan for the upcoming months. This she often referred to as her tickler file. Her predecessor had left her sketchy monthly folders with some additional e-mail files. She spent numerous hours in her first few weeks trying to look ahead to October and beyond as she pieced together the district's history. She didn't want to disrupt what was going well while she then integrated her vision for the future in these small daily events and in more systemic initiatives. Once again, Lily couldn't say enough about being organized. She felt it best to make the chaos more doable, and even sometimes fun. She also turned this tickler file into an electronic version for future use.

Thanks to Dr. Jim Merrins, executive program director of the Oswego State University Superintendent Development Program (SDP), and their candidates and faculty, sample entry plans and helpful materials may be found at www.superintendentofschools.com. Aspiring and current superintendents should utilize this information as they prepare for the many school leadership tasks that lie ahead.

IN A NUTSHELL

- Superintendents' individual beliefs form a basis for their vision of the school district they lead.
- A school superintendent's vision, whatever it may be, is held passionately, emotionally, and almost spiritually.
- Student needs are the focal point of a superintendent's vision.
- To promote the vision, superintendents maintain a high visibility at both district and school community events.
- Superintendents reap rewards when children under their watch achieve success.
- Superintendents are truly Keepers of the Dream. That is an enormous responsibility and task to perform.

- Successful superintendents are organized Keepers of the Dream.
- They develop an entry plan to ensure that the dream comes to fruition and they keep on track.

NAVIGATING THE POLITICS AND THE LAW

It was clear to Marcy that coming from out of state might be a factor in her new superintendency. Her husband had been transferred, and they made a decision that this time she would follow him. He had followed her to her previous superintendency. It was a second marriage for both, and with children grown and out of the house, their willingness and ability to move was different than it had been. Marcy had not anticipated that her experience outside the state would become an issue. Weren't there standards and assessments in all states? Didn't everyone want students to be successful regardless of from which side of the Mississippi or the Mason Dixon line they came?

All went well for the honeymoon period in which Marcy began to get to know the stakeholders. She had an entry plan that she shared with the board, and they seemed supportive. The entry plan dealt with ways in which she would meet stakeholders within the community and the schools. It dealt with the big picture of vision and getting everyone on board to truly make a difference for students. It had ideas for garnering more support from the community and legislators who had historically been more supportive of higher-profile school districts.

Then the real issues hit. The board president told her that the teachers were using too many printer cartridges and paper. What was she going to do about it? Some teachers still had coffee pots and microwaves in their classrooms. What was her plan to get rid of them? The bus drivers still clocked in for their coffee time and they shouldn't be paid for that time. How was she going to resolve this? And the list continued of small, yet caustic, issues that she was being asked to address as the board avoided all of her attempts to finalize a district mission, review a district improvement plan for a district on the state list for needing improvement, address the proposals for closing one of the elementary schools, and provide information for the negotiations of all bargaining units' contracts open simultaneously.

Marcy was caught in a bind. If she didn't address these issues, the board would be critical. If she did, she would clearly enter into a relationship with the teachers and transportation workers that would set the stage for her time in the district. She gently forged ahead and it cost her much support from these stakeholders. The board was also still critical that she didn't do enough and didn't do it fast enough. The issues came up during negotiations, and she is now struggling to stay afloat. Her lack of success with these issues was mentioned in her mid-year evaluation.

In finally talking with her mentor, she wished she had had the conversation earlier. Marcy's ability to multitask got her into trouble. Rather than sitting back and observing, she jumped into several situations that she would have been better off avoiding until she knew more about the organization. Had she taken more time to *get to know the stakeholders and observe the connections and interactions* among these individuals, alternate ways of achieving the same end results may have surfaced.

Marcy did pull back and took things more slowly, building connections and allies in the district. She spent a great deal of time communicating with her board. She made connections while at the grocery store, at church, and at the beauty salon. Her board president, and now her beautician, has come around and is seeing the need to focus on the big picture a bit more.

As for the larger political scene, Marcy has attended statewide superintendent conferences located in the same city as the state capital. She has attended workshops on working with her legislators and visited them when she attended the conference and at other times during the year.

Marcy talked about waiting until later in her career before becoming a superintendent. Raising her children was her first priority, but being turned off by what she believed to be the inherent politics in the position was another key factor for waiting, and actually for almost not taking the leap altogether. Now as a superintendent in her second position, she is glad she waited because keeping abreast of all of the nuances of political situations, large and small, can be exhausting.

For Linda, however, these challenges are invigorating. She loves devising ways to deal with these political issues. She likes problem solving ways to keep all stakeholders content. She enjoys developing ways to

overcome potential problems and reach a win-win with her stakeholders. Her advice is to not engage in overt political repartee but stay visible
and accessible.

Tips for contacting lawmakers are provided by many (Bassi, DeHoff,
& Hopson, 2004). They first suggest having real interaction with local
legislators and state representatives and senators. The connection between the legislators and finance people will be particularly important
during the budget process. When Marcy would contact her legislators
about a bill, she had the correct bill number and provided an executive
summary of her side of the issue. Although the vote may not always go
the way that best suits the district, it is wise to *keep a good relationship*.
It is important to be knowledgeable and involved in this process. When
establishing and maintaining credibility, legislators will also be more
inclined to listen.

There is political pressure to reside in the school district for many superintendents, male and female. Stakeholders prefer their superintendent to live and pay taxes in the district. If the superintendent does not
live in the district it often becomes an issue when budgets go down and
residents can say, "Well, you don't have to live here and pay these high
taxes." In Canada, Wallin (2001) found that there was a difference in the
pressure to live in the district between those who were superintendents
in booming districts and those in depressed and stable communities. In
these latter communities there was more political pressure to live in the
district.

Leah eventually resigned from her position as superintendent when
the board decided to enforce the residency requirement after she had
been in the position for a year. This is a similar scenario to one highlighted in *The School Administrator* (Goens, 2005). In their example,
Bill resigned so the board could focus attention on getting the bond
referendum passed. Bill found it extremely difficult to find another
position because he was not currently in one. However, Leah held on
to her position until she could find another one. It was much easier to
move to a new position from a superintendency rather than from being
unemployed.

Both Janice, from this same article noted above, and Marcy faced a
personnel change in the board from the board that had hired them. All
it takes is one powerful board member to change the entire political

dynamics of the board. In Janice's case, the new board member wanted her to hire a friend. In Marcy's case, the board member insisted and persuaded the rest of the board to give tenure to a relative who otherwise would not have been granted tenure. Janice eventually lost her position, while Marcy is still holding on by a thread. Janice's attorney was willing to advocate on her behalf, and she was successful in obtaining another school leadership position. There may be an emotional cost for "hanging in there."

Regardless of whether a superintendent stays or the contract is bought out, it is better if a superintendent does not assume the role of victim (Goens, 2005). Victims believe themselves to be powerless and impotent. Real players look for what responsibility is theirs and take it. They look for what can be changed as a result of what happened and then make it happen. They reflect on better ways to handle situations in the future and how to *see it coming* more clearly.

To move on, these superintendents need to learn to forgive themselves and others. This is all part of the healing process. Trying not to dwell on the situation and focusing on the future can help. Allowing others in may also help to get through this process. This is a good time to contact search consultants or networks for the next steps. And finally, be reflective and learn from the situation. Seek help from others but be respectful of their busy schedules.

Superintendents should be careful not to find themselves in a situation where they are pitted against another superintendent. Reeves (2004) cites a situation in Arkansas in which superintendents came to be at great odds with each other. She indicated that it is to everyone's advantage to try to find a middle ground and have a united front on issues. She cites William Bosher's "Six T's of Public Advocacy." Bosher is dean of public policy and education at Virginia Commonwealth University. His Six T's can be helpful to those aspiring to the superintendency. They are the following:

1. Talk: Build this communication and establish strong relationships.
2. Touch: Make personal appeals and help them understand the issues.
3. Tout: Look for those with influence and solicit votes.

4. Tally: Keep tabs on their votes and prepare a report card for the public.
5. Temper: Maintain your integrity and be known for your practice, not your politics.
6. Thank: Whether or not you have won, thank them.

When Juanita was dealing with parents who did not want to close their local elementary school, she utilized many of the elements suggested by Mizrahi and Gibson (2004). She made sure she was credible and knew her facts and the history of the building and enrollment projections. She approached the parents with empathy and emotion and truly listened to hear their concerns. She knew her goal was to make them as comfortable and supportive as possible about closing the school but that she would need to say no to their demands for it to remain open.

Juanita did not go against the board's directive even though she knew she might be, probably would be, the scapegoat for others' anger. She tried to be supportive of the parents and convey information and steps in a very linear and logical format in repeated venues. Ultimately, the building was closed and the parents and students adjusted to the new setting, which was safer and had great access to technology and nature. The school building that closed was converted into senior apartments and created revenue for the district. It was a long process but one that Juanita would feel good about leading.

Linda Was a Legal Leader

Linda's mentor had been astute in telling her what she needed to know regarding the law, legal processes, and legal ramifications of her decisions and the decisions and rights of the district. When she left her principalship, her staff gave her an immense copy of the school law book for her state. She thought it an odd gift until she realized that one of her teachers sat on the board of a neighboring district and knew she might be needing to bone up a bit before she began the job. Until now, she had been able to handle building-level situations with legal implications fairly successfully, knowing she could always call the superintendent if something got sticky. Now she was that superintendent.

In her school law course for superintendents, Cantu (2007) includes topics she knows will be necessary for superintendents in the state of Texas (www.tea.state.tx.us). The class addresses such issues as legal duties of superintendents, accountability and school finance, school admissions, employment, religion and prayer in schools, free speech, student discipline, public information laws, Federal Educational Rights and Privacy Act (FERPA), administrator immunity from suit, and voting rights including accessibility of voting places to persons with disabilities.

These topics are included in many current references for school law (Alexander & Alexander, 2008; Valente & Valente, 2005; Yudof, Kirp, Levin, & Moran, 2002) and an understanding of these was critical for Linda to feel confident in this realm. She knew when to call their school attorney, and it seemed there were so many nuances on the law that rather than err, she made the call. She did, however, have the vocabulary to talk intelligently about the issue (Schimmel, Fischer, & Stellman, 2008.) She could then understand some of the specific legal jargon that was a part of the response. Linda realized the gift she received when she left the principalship was not such a silly or impractical one after all.

IN A NUTSHELL

- Take time to observe and get to know the stakeholders before making changes.
- Find the district and community historians, both positive and negative, and solicit their accounts of previous decisions and current issues.
- Don't believe everything you hear.
- Use your network for connecting with local and state politicians—a personal introduction does a great deal to create this connection.
- Build strong allies in all political areas and with all groups of stakeholders.
- Have a knowledgeable advocate if you are not successful in one position so you can secure another.

- Be a player, not a victim. When something happens, look at your responsibility for the situation and for the resolution.
- Keep a good relationship with all legislators and establish and maintain your own credibility.
- Know the law and legal processes that impact you and your district.

KNOWING THE BUDGET BASICS

Kathleen Wood (her real name), superintendent of the Harpursville Central School District and adjunct professor at Cortland State University and Binghamton University, shared some of her thoughts about budget basics. She comes from a background as a school business official. Knowing the school budgeting processes and school finance is imperative to the success of a superintendent (Odden & Picus, 2007). While Kathleen's insights related to other topics are also included in other parts of this book, below are some of her tips about the budget.

Do not relinquish control to the business official. Kathleen began a bit tongue in cheek with recounting her experiences. She does not have the formal educational pedagogy coursework that is required to be a teacher. With that said, when she embarked on the path of readying herself to become a superintendent candidate, she knew that she would need to come up to speed quickly in the area of instruction. So, with assistance from her mentor, she developed a purposeful plan to close the gap in her learning.

Kathleen doesn't often see that same process with superintendent candidates who come with that rich instructional background but are weak in business administration. They take perhaps one required administrative course in finance and budget but typically leave it at that. In spite of her best attempts to tell them that they must immerse themselves in the business side of the business of education, they don't. And, they end up relinquishing control to their business administrator.

As a business administrator she can tell you that having someone totally defer to your judgment would be her dream come true. She could build her unrestricted fund balance; she could create reserves and fund them; she could cut off appropriations in November and could restrict how and when purchases were made, all without the superintendent really knowing it. She could force the budget to drive all curricular decisions, especially if her superintendent did not know the nuances of school finance, let alone anything about the business office functions. While this did not happen in her district, she is aware that this may take place in others—all because the superintendent shies away from the work of really knowing about the ins and outs of school business.

She stated that this did not happen in her district, but she will share that there was a different and, in retrospect, disturbing occurrence that could have and should have been avoided. Until she was invited into an administrative meeting, she was an untapped resource as the business official.

It is essential to have a trusting relationship with your business official, but it is also important to have firsthand knowledge of business basics so you can ask questions that need to be asked in order to maintain checks and balances with whomever is doing the day-to-day work.

All decisions are financial. Once she was included in the district's administrative teams meetings, Kathleen simply listened to try to gain an understanding of the dynamics of the group and tried to catch on to the language of education. As she listened, she heard some great ideas being shared (along with the more mundane "administrivia"), but many of these lofty plans stayed just that because the administrative team did not know where the money was to fund these ideas. This was especially true if the budget was already in place and it was the middle of the fiscal year. Their perception was that initiatives that were not on the table at budget voting time would have to be shelved until the following year.

The budget is nothing more than a blueprint. However, she knew where she had some discretionary appropriations that cushioned the budget. She knew that she had understated revenues so that she could recommend budget expansion (in some limited circumstances) or build on her fund balance. Kathleen knew that what she had in reserves would be able to accommodate initiatives in subsequent budgets without driving up the tax levy. Equally important, she knew what she had in funds other than the general fund that could supplement or supplant initiatives being predominantly or solely funded in the general fund. When the business side of the business of education was allowed full access to the instructional side, great things began to happen. She then became a true partner in the district's administrative team.

By sitting at the administrative table as the business official and being accepted as an administrator, by immersing herself in learning about instruction and curriculum, and with the help of her mentor who was then her superintendent, the school district's leadership team was able to allow the curriculum and instruction to drive the budget.

Yes, the residents approved a spending plan, but it was the bottom line they approved. Once the administrators were able to work as a cohesive team, that huge disconnect between business and instruction was bridged. She could move some funds around to support instructional initiatives.

Kathleen indicated that she is aware this process is not the same for urban districts and may not be similar to readers' districts' process where budget voter approval is not required. Finding out the process in one's home district would be an excellent place to begin.

Kathleen found that one of the biggest shocks that teachers learn is that funds can be moved around between budget lines, with some exceptions. They may believe they cannot ask for funds mid-year. They are usually told no. To her, that is an absolute sin. Unless a district is in a contingency budget, or under some other kind of financial crisis, there *should* be money. Budgeting so tight as to not allow mid-year wiggle room is simply unacceptable. Although they cannot ask that their textbook money be transferred to an account so they can have a teaching assistant, there are flexible alternatives for other needs.

So, what does the superintendent really need to know? A superintendent doesn't need to be an accountant but she or he does need to be kept apprised of the financial condition of the district on a routine basis. In addition to having the business official at weekly administrative meetings, the superintendent should be having a weekly meeting, one-to-one, with the business official. This could be used to really get a picture of the school district.

While initially wanting to use this time to become accustomed to the accounting system that the district is using, the superintendent is looking at information at the macro level. In other words, start with how the revenues compare to the expenses monthly, biannually, and so on.

The superintendent needs to ask, "Where is the cushion in the budget and how much cushion is there?" Look at federal pass-through funds, universal prekindergarten (UPK) monies, and other state grants. Does the district have any other grants that have a *shelf life*, or are they perpetual? Who and/or what expenses are allocated to these grants? At any time, a grant may be reduced or simply eliminated, and all expenses paid for with this grant money will have to be either shifted or eliminated.

Does the district have a district improvement plan or some other planning document that guides the district for the academic year? If not, develop one. Better yet, model the template after a district known for best practice in this process. The district needs a plan that is the blueprint to identify the initiatives that the district plans on directing their resources into. Without a plan, the superintendent could easily be seduced into redirecting resources into a myriad of different directions, thereby running the risk of marginalizing the success of any of the initiatives. Follow the established plan, and if other great ideas emerge, place them under consideration for next year.

There are reasons to deviate from a plan that was crafted in an environment of consensus with the stakeholders. Health and safety considerations are two reasons. Another reason to deviate is a state-directed mandate that emerges suddenly and is unfunded. Yes, that happens.

Superintendents need to know what reserves the district has and how they are funded. Superintendents would love to hear that due to a deliberate plan of underbudgeting revenues and underspending expenses, the district is continually replenishing or building on its reserves. That is fiscal responsibility to the school district.

Regional or intermediate unit aid-ability can be a superintendent's friend. Kathleen works in a relatively poor district. Her intermediate unit aid ratio is such that for every dollar she spends, the district gets back eighty cents in aid the following year. When her teachers want to go on field trips, she has the field trip expenses run through the intermediate unit, thereby reducing trip expenses to a fraction of the cost. If Kathleen and her leadership team want to offer professional development for their teachers and other staff, again, she runs the costs through this intermediate unit. By doing this she can offer top-flight programs and the necessary follow-up that will ensure the staff has support to fully implement any initiatives.

In other words, as superintendent, she really needs to have an understanding of how this intermediate unit aid works, and then have someone who will be knowledgeable enough to tease through the details for her. Many times, her first question is, "Can we get aid on this?" Even if the district only gets fifty cents back on the dollar, that is still beneficial. This aid does not come through until the following year, which means districts may have to front the money to start the ball rolling, but it is well worth that original investment. This process may look different in different states but it is one to investigate.

This process again may be different for urban or other districts that do not vote on their budgets. The key is to have a good handle on all aid ratios. New superintendents may do well to avail themselves of professional development opportunities in these fiscal areas, such as those offered by AASA affiliates in each state (www.aasa.org) or specific programs such as Fiscal Navigation offered by Superintendentofschools.org.

If a district decides to take back a program from the intermediate/regional unit to save money, that is fine. However, is the loss in regional unit revenue anticipated as well? If a district goes down that path, that question must be asked. Earlier, we mentioned that Kathleen's district gets eighty cents back on every dollar spent. To clarify this, there are some intermediate unit programs for which that is not the case. So, a superintendent needs to be very clear and very specific as to what programs are being considered to be removed from this umbrella and what the financial impacts in the current year and the subsequent fiscal year are relative to the loss of this aid.

Get to know categorical aid and transportation. Certain areas of appropriations are supported by aid that is directly aimed at those expenses in specific areas. For example, textbook aid in Kathleen's state is determined by a dollar figure per student. If her district does not expend the total amount that is allocated per student, the district doesn't get the aid. One year, she did not generate expenses to agree with the revenues that could be allocated. Her aid for textbooks was cut. That only happened once.

Transportation aid in her state and type of district is determined at a specific rate but is based upon what specific expenses occurred in the budget category called transportation. She raised this issue because field trips, band trips, sports outings, and daily transportation are all funded in this category. In her district, Kathleen gets ninety cents back on every dollar they spend. So, in light of the intermediate unit/regional aid, she has no reason to turn down any field trip. And they don't unless it does not have a link with the curriculum.

What you don't know, you don't know. Kathleen made several erroneous decisions regarding her perceptions of what teacher training and professional development were. Despite the fact that she had been with the organization for ten years prior to becoming the superintendent, she didn't realize that much of the professional development centered around content rather than pedagogy to improve the delivery of instruction. She was surprised to find, for example, that although some teachers were certified to teach English, they did not have the skills to teach literacy, which she envisioned as a key component of English Language Arts.

This was just one of her many "ah ha!" moments during the superintendency. So she learned never to assume anything. If it struck her as being odd, it probably was. In other words, trust your instincts. She shares this with others but takes it one step further. Ask questions, check for understanding, and be *curious*. There is always room to be reflective and add to leadership knowledge to know both the art and science of integrating this information into leadership practice (Seivert & Cavaleri, 2005).

Get to know the jargon. In an environment where literacy is a cornerstone of the educational process, school administrators are nuts about creating and using acronyms and coded phrases. She once sat in on a meeting that sounded something like this, "At the latest CSE meeting, DSS was there and they had lawyered up. So, we agreed to do a FBA and to continue OT and PT in a stay-put provision but of course, Mom won't be satisfied." What does this mean?

Of course, it means at the last Committee on Special Education (CSE), the Department of Social Services (DSS) sent a representative and that the family had secured the advice or services of a lawyer. The committee agreed to conduct a Functional Behavior Analysis (FBA) and to continue providing Occupational Therapy (OT) and Physical Therapy (PT), which by law in this state, we must continue (stay-put provision) until the results of the FBA are determined. Mom really means the mother. They wanted to do the right thing for the student but were caught up in the jargon and the process.

Never assume that you know what the jargon is. When exploring the job, as part of your data collection, ask if there is a new board of education (BOE) member handbook. This will most likely contain all of the commonly used jargon, acronyms, and local phrases that are used in that district. It will likely be a user-friendly handbook, as it is used by that school's board of education. In addition, ask questions. A new superintendent can always pull the *rookie* card in the first year with the phrase, "I am not familiar with that phrasing from my previous district. What does it mean?"

The business side of education is no different from any other business. In fact, without any central office experience, it will be a real challenge to navigate not only the language of school business but the nuts and bolts of the operations. When meeting with the school business official, have her or him break down all abbreviations, acronyms, and coded phrases. Quite frankly, this is a good exercise for the school business official as well. Simply put, ask questions.

Get all of the information. As part of the preparation for the interviewing process, it is important to gather as much information about the district as possible. Have a list of the essential business and financial documents that will help inform and guide your decisions in your first foray into a district.

What are the essential documents? Request any union contracts and any board of education policy book, plus any plans that are mandated by the district as well as any nonmandated plans. Such plans might be a technology plan, a district-improvement plan, or an annual athletic plan. Secure the official minutes from three or four board of education meetings. Three or four editions of the latest school newsletter will help the new superintendent get a flavor of the culture of the district also.

Include the latest budget—not necessarily the budget document that is presented to the public, as it may not reveal the essential nuts and bolts of the finances. What would be asked for is a copy of the current year budget; the prior year budget; and if available, the prospective budget and the actual revenues and expenditures from the prior year. Additionally, a new superintendent should request a copy of the audited financial statements from the previous two years.

Gathering these types of essential documents will give a picture of the district. Does the spending plan support the various action plans (e.g., the district improvement plan, technology plan) or is the spending plan driving every other decision with the plans being either a response to a mandate or some good ideas? Is the district in sound financial condition according to the external auditors? If there were items cited as needing improvement, were they corrected or are they ongoing?

Union contracts are chock full of financial obligations. Contracts sometimes also contain some very unique language that can be a knee-jerk reaction to something that occurred at some point in the history of the district. Language that is very specific in this manner is difficult to remove from contracts, as there is usually emotional baggage that is tied to it. Time and trust can aid in the modification or removal of this potentially problematic wording. A read of contracts can also reveal a functional or dysfunctional current and/or historical relationship between the bargaining units and the district.

Overall, what these essential documents reveal is a dissection of the issues that required input and consideration from what should have been a cross-section of the stakeholders of the district. Moreover, it informs the reader of any potential pitfalls or challenges that may lie ahead.

By the way, a school district employee is most likely responsible for amassing this body of documents that have been requested. Find out who it is and send the appropriate thank-you note. It is likely that this person is an influential member of the school community. Plus, after all of that work, he or she deserves the special acknowledgment.

Superintendents agree that it is imperative that they know the language and basics of school finance to be successful. Key elements of the budgeting process (Owings & Kaplan, 2005) and general school finance (Odden & Picus, 2007) allow superintendents to be more confident in their role as CEO of the districts they lead.

IN A NUTSHELL

- Know the basics of school business so you are not dependent upon your business official.

- Remember that all decisions are financial.
- The budget is nothing more than a blueprint.
- Have ongoing meetings with your business official; schedule weekly meetings so time doesn't slip by.
- Look at state aid and other forms of aid for funding.
- Consider and then reconsider taking back any programs to the district from a regional provider.
- Know about categorical aid and transportation.
- Admit what you don't know.

ENHANCING BOARDSMANSHIP

When Marcy assumed her superintendency, she was shocked to discover that the board that had supported her when she was a teacher and principal in the same district was now becoming public enemy number one. They had hired her for the position as superintendent but were starting off their relationship on a very contentious note.

Marcy brought in a consultant to help facilitate the development of board and superintendent goals. She brought in another consultant to facilitate a dialogue about the board's role in supporting instruction and helping to create a culture of literacy. The friction continued.

When she did as they directed, she was accused of being too assertive or masculine. When she held back, she was accused of not being masculine enough. How did she address this ongoing conflict? She stepped down. Despite what the board had indicated at the outset, they now had to backpedal when she took care of the issues they had instructed her to address. She had cleaned things up as requested, and now, with the ire of the community heating up, they needed a scapegoat. Marcy was that person.

The lessons to be learned were to never forget the importance of the match. The match looks different when one is a teacher or principal. The match is critical in a relationship where the rubber meets the road and the superintendency is where it does.

A second lesson was to have a heightened awareness when the board says they would like you to come in and clean up a few things. This may

mean that once this is accomplished and the ire of staff and the community is raised, someone has to pay; that person may well be you.

A final lesson for Marcy was to never forget to keep lines of communication open. She ought to have known earlier that one of her colleagues
could barely tolerate her being her principal when Marcy moved into
that position. When she moved to the superintendency the jealousy was
even more intolerable for this teacher, and she started to undermine
Marcy's decisions. A former friend and ally was now a major nemesis.

The board-superintendent relationship can be a very tenuous and
tension-filled one, as we have just seen above. It also may be one that
works well. Lawrence (2005) outlines some guiding principles for effective board-superintendent relationships.

The school board has the right to be supported by the superintendent
but on the other hand, the superintendent has the right to be supported
by the board. In this political relationship, does the superintendent truly
have the right to expect this support? Does she model this respect and
support of her board first? Does she assume responsibility for the tough
decisions or try to pass them off on her board?

Jane knew that she would take the heat when she suspended five students for vandalism in the cafeteria. The students had come into school
after hours and spray painted numerous ceiling tiles and overturned
chairs and tables in the cafeteria. They were observed by the custodian
and jeered at him when he told them he was calling the police. He didn't
call the police; he called the superintendent. By the time she arrived
the students had left, but the custodian could identify each student; this
is the advantage of a small school. Conversely, the advantage can also
be the disadvantage. In a small district everyone knows everyone, and
several of the students were Jane's neighbors' children.

Suspension wouldn't have been as difficult had it not involved graduation. She believed that the students should not be allowed to participate
in the graduation ceremony. The parents protested that the students
had never been in trouble before and after all, this was just their senior
prank. Jane held firm, but her decision was overturned by the board.

Feeling that she was not supported and that this decision set a very
poor example for other students, she met with the board. It was clear
to her that they were not going to see the situation her way, especially
because one of the students was a board member's niece.

The students were required to each write a note of apology and set up a plan to pay for the nearly $2,000 in damages to the cafeteria. They also had to write a note to the teaching staff that would now need to create a new final exam schedule because the cafeteria was not an option for exams.

On graduation day, Jane handed these students their diplomas and wondered what these students and their peers had learned. Had they learned that they can be irresponsible and not have consequences for their behavior? Had they learned that because of their economic and white privilege they would not be held accountable? And what had Jane learned? She had learned that the board's support was not there for her. She was a new superintendent and had to weigh the benefits of most days in the district with this more extreme example. She learned that a right is only a right when both parties' behavior is congruent with the assumed right. She learned that she must continue to ask herself the question, "For what (issue, decision) am I willing to lose my job?" This time she decided to stay.

An after note: soon after this incident, it was time for the school board to have a contract negotiations conversation with Jane. As a result of this incident, the board wrote in her evaluation that she was a team player and offered her a substantial raise. She felt awkward accepting the raise but wrote in her reflection to the board that she would like to schedule a retreat later in the summer so they could agree on the core values upon which they would form future decisions. The retreat took place, but the conversation regarding these core values and decision making were addressed very briefly.

Eileen dealt with the situation of whether or not to become involved in helping to recruit a candidate for a board vacancy. McKay and Peterson (2004) interviewed superintendents regarding this issue. Eileen's choice to show discretion when soliciting potential board members was supported by the veteran superintendents cited in this research. According to the research there is no consensus regarding becoming directly involved. However, to not be involved in soliciting potential board candidates may not be in one's best interest.

To be successful with her board, Juanita planned the board agenda with her board president. She was clear that it was the board's meeting and given that, this collaborative approach was highly effective

(Townsend, Johnston, Gross, Lynch, Garcy, Roberts, & Novotney, 2007). Equally important for Juanita and her board president was to plan to review the meeting either later that night or the next day. Kimball (2005) also suggests that the relationship with the board president should not preempt the superintendent's relationship with the entire board. Juanita prepared a weekly update for her board and gave special attention to ensure that her board president knew more of the details to help him answer questions from parents and the community should they arise at the board meeting.

Juanita tried to help her board stay true to their roles. The board's charge is to make policy; hers is to implement board policy and develop regulations that reflect the board's policies. Together they plan and establish organizational goals, and she sets her goals accordingly. The board should engage in ongoing self-assessment and adopt standards for conducting board meetings and communication to all stakeholders.

With regard to administration and personnel, the board hired Juanita and should delegate personnel matters to her. While Juanita recommends teachers for appointment and tenure, the school board officially hires school staff and grants tenure. The board evaluates the superintendent and the superintendent is responsible for evaluating the staff. Juanita or her designee negotiates employee contracts based upon guidelines set by the board. The board ratifies these agreements.

Juanita recommends budgetary priorities after discussion with the board. She also makes recommendations for renovation and construction needs. The board has approval over all these items. She ensures the facilities are maintained and the board oversees this.

Juanita views herself as an instructional leader. She recommends program changes, initiatives, and curricular evaluations. She keeps the board informed and they approve any textbook, curriculum, or program changes.

Juanita and her board share a responsibility for creating, implementing, and evaluating a communication process that reaches all stakeholders. The process needs to be efficient, effective, and inclusive of all members of the community. This communication, when it works smoothly within the district and the community, can make an important difference in the culture and success of the district.

Six themes emerged from the conversations with these superintendents about their relationships with school board members. Many of the suggestions made by Juanita were supported in Ivory and Acker-Hocevar's book *Successful School Board Leadership: Lessons from Superintendents* (2007). Dave Else, director of the Institute for Educational Leadership, captures some of these in a monograph he wrote regarding strengthening school board-superintendent relationships (2000).

1. Develop clear roles and expectations. Clarify the role with the board prior to accepting the position. Make sure there is ongoing support and training for new board members and clarity for those running for the board regarding the parameters of the role. Align superintendent evaluations with these roles and ensure that these roles are visible to the entire community.

2. Work together to develop the vision for the district. Make sure the right people are at the table to develop this vision. Ensure participation with all stakeholders. Be mindful of the role that climate and culture play in carrying out this vision. Seek to clarify the purpose of the school and values of the community and school board prior to developing the vision.

3. Establish a climate of mutual trust and respect. There are many superintendents who have annual board retreats to help the board clarify their goals, vision, and communication process. School board organizations and consultants are readily available to help facilitate these retreats. These retreats help to engender trust and minimize distractions. Having a united and collaborative approach to issues helps to garner support from the community. Revisit the board's policy handbook and review the board's code of ethics and roles. Provide ongoing support and mentoring for board members and model respect and ethical decision making at all times.

4. Establish consistent communication. Whether it is the board packets that go out via snail mail or e-mail, the morning phone calls with the board president the morning after the board meeting, or the explicit rule that board members redirect concerns from parents and community members to the appropriate administrator, there can never be enough said about effective communication.

Newsletters and websites with collaborative articles written by the superintendent and the board send a message of unity to the community. There should be ongoing checks to make sure that the communication systems that were put into place are still the most effective mechanisms for current communication. Having the board agree to ground rules for communication, such as they will read their e-mail daily, are helpful. Create communication vehicles so all board members receive information at the same time.

5. Set the stage for effective decision making. Take another look at the culture of the district to help promote decisions that will empower all stakeholders and involve the board in a meaningful way. Encourage and model open-mindedness during all decision-making opportunities. Devise ways for board members to defuse sessions in which decision making may be contentious or passionate. Engage in conflict resolution strategies and arrange for board training, if necessary.

6. Develop and maintain effective connections with the community. Ethical behavior is a must when dealing with the community. They need an honest representation of the facts. Strive to have communication come from an original source and have several iterations in between. Step out of the comfort zone to belong to organizations in the community that may be unfamiliar.

The board-superintendent relationship is the most critical relationship for the success of a superintendent. Ideally, the superintendent and the school board work collaboratively for the health and well-being of the school district and its community.

IN A NUTSHELL

- The superintendent's best ally is a school board president who has been kept well informed.
- Involving the board in training or a retreat can help to unify the board and solidify their positions on key issues, goals, and vision/mission.

- Clarifying board and superintendent roles helps to move initiatives along.
- Engaging in a collaborative communication effort benefits the board, the superintendent, and all stakeholders within the school district community.
- The superintendent may support aspects of productive board of education involvement in such areas as the following:
  - annual review and setting of goals
  - annual evaluations
  - policy review and development
  - review and approval of fiscal activity
  - appointment, review, tenure, and termination of personnel
  - annual review, development, and approval of five-year plans
  - receipt of reports
  - orientation of new board members

WORKING WITH THE MEDIA AND PUBLIC RELATIONS

Dee Dee got a call from the local newspaper while she was dealing with a situation in which one of the district's beloved teachers was being accused of sexual harassment. She had discussed the situation with the district's attorney and was clear what she should and shouldn't say to the media. However, not returning their call was not an option. She did not want the district to be quoted as having "no comment." She knew it was better to call the paper back immediately.

Lily was home for the first night in a week when she got a call from her elementary school principal. The bus drivers were out on strike and they were picketing just beyond the front steps while she was welcoming parents to their fall Open House. The principal had the situation under control until the media showed up. She knew the policy for the district was that the superintendent was the official spokesperson and thus she called Lily. Lily took off her jeans and donned her professional wear to head out to the school. She knew this required her to be present to help all those involved feel supported and heard.

Barbara was retiring from her district. Her board was involved in selecting her successor. The local newspaper had a reputation for putting a negative spin on the activities of her district. They had contacted her regarding the progress of the search. When she indicated that she would not share whatever information she had, the journalist called the board president who was livid that the paper was trying to obtain the names of the finalists. His response was curt and he hung up on the reporter. This caused another article to be written that did not paint the board or the superintendent in the best light. As tough as the reporter had been, hanging up the phone is never a good alternative.

Melissa's small local newspaper seemed to get a new journalist every six months. She learned several years ago not to assume that the journalist was trying to depict her district poorly for the purpose of selling papers. These new journalists didn't know about education. They made numerous erroneous assumptions that proved to cost her time and energy to mend fences with a variety of stakeholders. Melissa learned that if she asked the reporter to repeat back to her what he or she heard, she had a much better chance of catching inaccuracies and enabling the reporter to write a factually sound article.

Maureen and Allison represent two very different philosophies regarding dealing with the media. Maureen likes to fly below the radar while Allison thinks it is best to be very present in front of the media. Maureen will call the media back when they call but has never called a press release for anything more public than the school play or groundbreaking for the new school. Allison, on the other hand, likes to call the media to share incremental progress on their building project, names of finalists for her principal positions, and stakeholder meetings outlining a new International Baccalaureate (IB) program they are investigating. Allison has the presence and skills to handle the press and use them as an asset. Maureen doesn't feel she has those skills and thus likes to keep the media at bay.

Beth is a new superintendent. She does not know the members of her community, including the press. She made appointments to go and visit members of her business and media community. She wanted to introduce herself, find out how they have collaborated in the past, and talk about ideas for the future. The time she took with this initial contact proved to be very beneficial for the district and for her personal career. She made contacts that helped the district receive support from the community. The press was also involved in covering some of these positive community events.

JoAnne is technologically savvy but does not have time to keep up with the latest iterations of new software and hardware. When she became a superintendent, she teamed up with a high school assistant principal who was into technology. They worked on the district website and helped teachers develop their own. The media of today extends beyond print and TV, and the more she believed she could use technology for the next generation, the more widespread her programs became. She encouraged staff to use the Web to gain more national and international access to current events and to share their knowledge using the Web as well. Together, JoAnne and the assistant high school principal also developed a district blog around the time of a referendum for a capital project.

The media can be a very valuable asset for the district. Engaging them right from the beginning of assuming the role of superintendent may bring about an effective *long-term collaborative relationship* (Hughes & Hooper, 2000).

The National School Public Relations Association (NSPRA) has many publications and recommendations for superintendents who want to engage in effective public relations and interactions with the media. Their website is www.nspra.org.

Recommendations from Newquist (2004) and from an interview with a superintendent search consultant Dr. William Silky were as follows:

- Return phone calls promptly. How are individuals made to feel welcome when they call your schools? Does your voice mail system allow callers to access the people they need without frustration? Dee Dee makes sure this happens, and when she hears of a staff member who is not courteous, she has a conversation about why and makes suggestions for change. She views her staff and herself as service employees to her students, parents, and community. She believes that her background and experience in the business world prior to becoming a teacher, principal, and then superintendent has done much to help her know how the public reacts.

- Notify stakeholders about meetings and events. Are your meetings accessible and are all stakeholders welcome? Is there time for the audience to ask questions? Is the community notified of school events? Are parents and community members given enough notice to make arrangements for child care or transportation? Is notification provided in languages other than English if necessary? Betty has teachers and community members who will translate her newsletters into several languages to match the needs of her parents and community.
- Ensure that teachers and administrators communicate with parents in a positive way. How are newsletters used? Face-to face communication? Phone communication? E-mail, blogs, or other technology? Whatever the modality, make sure the information is relevant and timely. Create documents from the perspective of the intended audience. Be careful that newsletters aren't too nice looking. Kathleen published a stunning color newsletter but was criticized that the district should not use funds this way. She needed to educate her public that she received state aid back and the newsletter was thus very economical.
- Pick up the phone and call the media about the good things happening. One school may get more coverage than another simply because they pick up the phone more readily. Make sure you subscribe to all the local newspapers and check the local TV and radio stations regularly to know their perspectives and biases. Check online chat rooms or blogs to know what is being said about the district.
- The National Association of Secondary School Principals (www .nassp.org) offers these great tips:
  - Create a list with the names and numbers of key media contacts in your community.
  - When you hear a national news story, contact the people on your press list and let them know how it is affecting your school. Reporters are always looking for ways to put a local twist on a national story.
  - News people love statistics so keep them handy. Use them to illustrate your perspective.
- Make sure you always communicate in a crisis. Whether it is large or small, be prepared to talk about it and have the facts right away.

Do whatever it takes so this doesn't get out of control. First, communicate with the staff and keep them informed. Next, communicate with parents. Jill keeps some letters ready to send home and an e-mail template that she can adapt to fit a range of emergency situations. This helps when a situation occurs at the end of the day and she wants something to go home with students to allay parents' concerns. She is ready to e-mail this to her parents as well. This is also shared with local media if she thinks the incident will draw media attention.

Jill has instructed her administrators and staff that she is the one district spokesperson and all media contact should be referred to her. She states the facts and provides as much information as possible to be clear and concise, thus avoiding rumors and speculation.

- Frances included some tips for talking with the media during a crisis:
  - Be careful of "off the record" and make sure whatever you say you are willing to see in print.
  - Keep the board informed of the press's involvement.
  - Speak slowly and don't say more than you need to. Let the reporter move the conversation past the silence.
  - Answer only the questions you want to answer and don't be pulled off topic.
  - Wait until you are calm or emotionally ready to talk with the press.
- Some additional steps to take within the first thirty minutes of a crisis that are suggested by the National School Public Relations Association (www.nspra.org) include:
  - Make sure you understand the circumstances; define the problem.
  - Consider the options; act decisively to ensure the health and safety of students and staff and protection of district property.
  - Communicate with all staff and parents as you can; keep the news media informed.
  - Create a crisis assessment and information sheet. Include this information:
    - your name
    - school

- time
- phone number
- fax number
- brief description of crisis
- number of people involved
- outsiders on site—for example, police, media, ambulance
- steps already taken by you
- anticipated next steps
- resources needed now—examples include media relations, medical aid, clerical assistance, law enforcement, psychological/social/guidance counselors, food service, communications, insurance/claims, legal aid, transportation, safety assistance, maintenance, and construction

All of these areas were worthy of consideration. Failure to project the right image for the media can be a superintendent's nightmare. It is better to be proactive and have the media on your side if at all possible. In Jane's hometown, it didn't matter what she did or what she said to the press about her district. They always mined for whatever the antithesis is of *gold*. At the end of her superintendency she still had not won them over and they continued to criticize the district.

IN A NUTSHELL

- It is better to call the media back immediately.
- There should be a clear policy regarding to whom the media will speak within your district. Who is your district spokesperson and what if this person isn't available?
- Although it is generally a good practice to call the media as soon as possible, make sure you are past being emotional or angry before placing the call or sending the e-mail.
- Help new reporters learn about education. Ask them to repeat back what they think they heard so you can check for accuracy.
- Know if you are a "fly below the radar" person or a "frequent press releases" person.

- Find different avenues to get to know your reporters, editors, TV/video connections, and Web masters.
- Remember to be sensitive and respectful to cultural, ethnic, racial, and gender factors when dealing with the media.

TRUSTING YOUR INTUITION

The big question was, "Whom do I trust?" Zoe had gone into the superintendent's position with her eyes wide open. She knew there were dangers and traps along this professional journey. Decisions of all types (financial, personnel, instructional, legal) needed to be made, but how would she know if the ones she made were the right decisions?

When she didn't know the answer, Zoe asked questions, lots of them. She was secure enough in her own abilities to realize that seeking assistance was not a sign of weakness. She knew going in that she didn't need to know every aspect of the job and all the decisions she would be called on to make. No one could possibly know everything, and she would be a fool to think that she did. Besides, she was a reasonably intelligent person, the epitome of a lifelong learner. What she did not know, she could learn. What she did realize was that her failure to ask for help might potentially lead to trouble and possible professional failure. Zoe did not want to go down that road.

Zoe had a long and storied professional life in educational leadership. She had come up through the ranks of teaching, had been selected as a teacher leader, and then gradually moved, after pursuing additional advanced degree program completion and state certification, into building and district leadership positions. As a teacher and as a school leader, Zoe had experienced many situations that had required split-second decision making and others where she could take some time to weigh the pros and cons of the situation at hand. She had credibility because of her career path and all her ensuing successes. Zoe had learned to trust her gut, and if the decision felt right, it probably was. She never hesitated to err on the side of the child. "What's best for children?" was her motto, and it never led her astray.

As a superintendent, Zoe answered, naturally, to her governing school board. Over the years, she learned to anticipate what each board member wanted, plus what the school board as a whole needed. Her past experiences, most of which were successful, helped her build the confidence necessary to trust her own self. She did, however, understand that some of her professional expertise grew out of the learning she gleaned from her failures. Sometimes failure is the best teacher.

Additionally, Zoe sought advice and counsel from professional colleagues and personal friends. Roberta, an experienced superintendent in a neighboring school district, possessed this terrific attitude. When Zoe called upon her, she often repeated that she always expected to be good and right. Roberta had a strong ego, and she helped colleagues build their own, too.

Samantha was Zoe's personal friend, having grown up together in the same neighborhood. Sam was quietly confident and regularly engaged in reflective practice. No matter what the issue, no matter what the situation, Samantha always stepped back and reflected on what she did, how she handled the situation, who benefited from the decision, and so on. Zoe sought her expertise often, almost as a cathartic way of dealing with some particularly difficult circumstances. Zoe's friend and colleague validated her intuition.

So, what can the aspiring superintendent learn from Zoe and her friends? *Learning whom to trust* is often the first step into a new superintendency. This discovery may take time. The leader at the top often has a lonely position. It is through patience, time, and the effort of building relationships that trust is learned and fortified. Being a two-way street, trust grows slowly and patiently.

The ability and regular practice of *asking questions* is a positive skill of a superintendent. An offshoot of figuring out whom to trust is developing the ability to figure out who among your colleagues can help you in any given situation. Networking, which has been detailed in chapter 2 of this book, is an excellent way of learning who knows what. Superintendents' cultivation of a support system at the professional level is priceless.

Superintendents must develop good *questioning skills*. Asking clarifying questions to understand the problem is a good starting point. Further questioning may help in decision making itself. What is the impact? Who will be affected? What am I missing? How will I communicate this decision when made? What if people do not understand? How will I address this? What will be my next step? All of these questions will assist a superintendent in the course of the everyday work.

Listening and observing are two traits that can help a superintendent. These traits should be used often, especially in a new job. Listening and observing assist a superintendent in beginning to *anticipate* the wants and needs of the school district community, its staff, students, and school board. Anticipation and an appropriate response are both tools that all superintendents need.

Trusting your intuition takes time. It takes individual learning from experiences that are successful and those that are unsuccessful. Oftentimes, the greater learning comes from one's failures than from one's successes. Superintendents' quest for learning and the positive attitude that potentially develops are great assets for professional consideration (Funk, 2004). This probably will occur over an extended period of time, perhaps over the school leaders' entire careers.

Developing a *support system* of professional colleagues, personal friends, and family is crucial to the role of a school superintendent (Williamson & Hudson, 2003). Professional colleagues are cultivated throughout a career. Personal friends may date all the way back to childhood. And, nothing can beat family support, which oftentimes keeps school leaders very grounded but surrounded with love and care.

Reflective practice should begin early on in a superintendent's career. Administrative interns, as a requirement of coursework and the internship itself, are often required to engage in this task while focusing on their early experiences in decision making. If done often enough, reflection can become a habit and a positive one at that. Looking at oneself and how one acts helps develop self-confidence, so very necessary to successfully lead today's schools.

It's interesting that we spend a great deal of time helping young students learn the five senses. What if we spent equal time practicing our sixth sense—intuition?

IN A NUTSHELL

- A first step is figuring out whom to trust.
- Superintendents should always ask questions and seek help when needed. This is not a sign of weakness.

- Learning to anticipate what the needs and wants of your constituency are will come with time, patience, and success.
- Superintendents do not need to know it all—ask, ask, ask.
- With confidence and an attitude of "I expect to be good," trusting your intuition becomes an easier task to manage.
- Successful school leaders surround themselves with good people: family, personal friends, and/or professional colleagues.
- Successful superintendents regularly engage in reflective practice.

HONING DECISION-MAKING SKILLS

A sitting superintendent mentored Yvonne as she journeyed through the search process. She listened and reflected on his guiding words, tucking them away for future reference. During the mentoring sessions, she repeatedly asked him questions, probing and clarifying for her own mind what was meant by what her mentor said. Yvonne knew she would draw on these words of wisdom throughout her career.

Yvonne started early in the superintendent search process, doing her homework on the school district she wanted to lead. She dug deep, looking for issues that were apparent and those that may have been kept hidden. Her thoroughness from the beginning helped her, especially in the early days—the honeymoon period—of the superintendency. While decision making is crucial at every juncture in the superintendency, the decisions made by those new to the position seem to be particularly scrutinized by many watchful eyes.

In addition to mentoring experiences and being thorough in preparing for a superintendent search, Yvonne's own professional and personal skills centered on her ability to build relationships. Professional relationships with people within her building, district, community, and/or neighboring school districts were a priority for Yvonne. She frequently drew on her strong people skills to forge relationships, which assisted her in making the right decision.

One important aspect of decision making that Yvonne's mentor stressed to her was to study the impact of the decisions she considered making. Gathering knowledge on a topic up front was directly related to studying the effects, both positive and negative, of the impact her decisions would have. Thinking through the impact of more minor decisions helped Yvonne hone her skills when it came to making decisions on a grander scale.

As a lifelong educator, Yvonne based her professional decisions on what was right for children. This occurred from the time she entered the teaching profession, and she was confident it would govern her until retirement. Who could argue with making a decision because it was good for children? Yvonne held children's best interests dear to her heart. She recognized that what she thought was best for children might vary from what others believed was best. That is why a dialogue among stakeholders is so important.

Yvonne was very learned and had many years of life and professional experiences. From time to time, however, Yvonne made a poor decision. When it became apparent that had happened, she stepped back and took input from others. Some criticism came uninvited. Some critical input she sought. Some was delivered anonymously and some was very public. Criticism comes with the territory in the superintendency. "The buck stops here" and "Uneasy lies the head that wears the crown" are both truisms regarding this top school leadership position (Harrington-Lueker, 2002).

Yvonne believed firmly in apologizing for mistakes made. She held herself accountable, as she knew others did of her also. She sought input to understand why it was the wrong decision and worked diligently to resolve the issue. In Yvonne's positive outlook on life, she viewed this situation as an opportunity to learn and grow both professionally and personally. She would get it right the next time.

Kathleen admits that teachers do put in long hours on the job. While acknowledging the time commitment of teachers, she tries to explain that the weight of the responsibilities between teachers and superintendents is enormously different. Leaders must sometimes make gut-wrenching decisions. Administrators must constantly keep their focus at the macro level but be able to dive to the micro level at a moment's notice.

Kathleen remembers the first time, within the first week actually of being a superintendent, that she was faced with a crisis. People were giving her the facts of the matter and then there was this silence. She realized that they were looking at her and to her for guidance and direction. At that moment, she felt panicked. Figuratively, Kathleen looked behind her, wondering who was making this decision? She realized it was her. It was her real step over the threshold to the superintendency.

Honing decision-making skills is key to a superintendent's professional journey. *Mentors play key roles* in the continuing development of school superintendents (Hammond, 2006). Their guidance and conveyance of wisdom are tools superintendents can use in decision making. Experience is oftentimes the best teacher, and this is no exception in the superintendency.

Superintendents should readily *use questioning techniques*. Knowing what to ask and whom to ask it of is a skill that develops over time. Questioning is a good habit to develop and refine throughout a superintendent's career.

The superintendency is a people person position. AASA (2006) suggests that leadership for change involves "having the heart to connect with people" (p. 9). *Relationship building can positively impact a superintendent's decision-making skills* (Williamson & Hudson, 2003). It is one rung on the ladder to leading a school district successfully.

The focus of all decisions made by a superintendent should be for the *benefit of the school district's children*. While oftentimes there exist competing agendas or conflicting interests, the school leader can successfully bring others to consensus by simply asking if what is to be decided is good for children. There can legitimately be little or no argument with that mantra as the sole decider of the impact a decision will make.

While no one likes to be wrong, it is important for superintendents to realize early on when a mistake has been made. Superintendents who hold themselves accountable for what they do are being professionally responsible. If they are wrong in some instance, the right thing to do is to *admit the mistake*. Covering it up or blaming others for the poor decision does not work and may come back to haunt the superintendent at a later date. An apology for the error is important. The resolve to fix what went wrong and to work hard to correct the situation lends itself to positive working relationships within a school district. That a superintendent would believe in and model this type of accountability helps ensure a viable, functioning school district.

IN A NUTSHELL

- Mentors can play a role in honing a superintendent's decision-making skills, whether the superintendent is new to the role or a veteran.
- All superintendents should make it a professional habit to ask questions for learning and clarification purposes.
- One of the keys to being a better decision maker is to forge relationships within your own constituency.
- Superintendents should study the impact of their decisions for all those possibly affected by the decision.
- Most of the time, it is just you, the superintendent, as the responsible party for decisions made.
- *Is this good for children?* should be the main thrust behind each decision made.
- If a poor decision is made, admit the mistake, apologize for the error, and work hard to make it right. Try very hard not to make the same mistake a second time.

CRAFTING SUPERINTENDENT EVALUATIONS

When Eileen was offered her first superintendent position she was told by the male board president that she was not to wear skirts to board meetings. Her legs were too attractive and would be distracting for the board. Eileen knew then and there that *the fit* wasn't there. She could have taken legal action but knew if she did she would never get another superintendency. She chose to decline their offer and went on to a very successful superintendency elsewhere. She let it go and hasn't forgotten. She says she will address this issue when she is in her last contract in her current district so she can't be hurt by the possible fallout. She continues to be active with a state organization for women in administration to help them work through similar issues and make decisions regarding what action to take.

To have the greatest success in her current district, Eileen has worked with the board to *align her goals with her evaluation from the board.* When she first arrived, the goals were primarily focused on management issues and the percentage of increase in test scores. She has altered that to reflect current research regarding effective leadership. Using the research findings of Marzano, Waters, and McNulty (2005) she has developed a few goals that are aligned with her vision and that of the board. These goals are observable and thus may be used for her evaluation. She is astute enough to know that no one will follow her leadership unless she also is a good manager, so she does pay critical attention to detail.

Another superintendent, Jill, has also developed a set of goals with her board that follow this same line of thinking. She has also worked with her leadership team to have their goals be similarly aligned. She believes that this alignment of goals puts energy and passion back into work.

In other research (Dana & Bourisaw, 2006) women identified factors in retaining their superintendency. Those who were successful in retaining their position noted the following: there was a fit between the superintendent and the board; the superintendent was able to learn about the community to assess the fit; the board was able to work as a team, and their level of function assisted the superintendent; the board did not micromanage; the board did not seek out the superintendents for issues of self-interest; the leadership team was supportive of the superintendent; and the *superintendents had excellent communication skills*, especially for reaching all stakeholders within the district and within the larger community. These items may comprise part of the superintendent's evaluation.

How do superintendents keep abreast of how their performance is being viewed by a variety of stakeholders? What methods are currently being used to evaluate superintendent performance? Here are a few cited by Glass and Franceschini (2007). Multiple methods of evaluation may have been used. Numbers reflect the percentage of sitting superintendents in their study who are being evaluated using a particular method:

1. Criteria created by board in advance   28.5%
2. Criteria agreed upon by board and superintendent   55.3%
3. Discussion between board and superintendent   50.0%
4. Discussion during executive session of board   49.3%
5. Written evaluation by board/board chair   72.4%

Janet talked about her evaluation and how she *didn't see it coming*. Her evaluation during her first year was excellent. She met with the board and they wrote an evaluation for her. Her second year, she was involved in an evaluation during executive session. During this session, board members expressed concerns that she was hearing for the first time. When she asked why board members had not talked to her previously about these issues they indicated that she should have known them.

Needless to say, she didn't, and during the summer they chose to buy out the third year of her contract. She was devastated at the lack of trust and willingness to be forthcoming that was demonstrated by the board and the community. She had been asked by the board to come in and "clean up a few things." She did just that, and when her work provoked the ire of the teachers' union and the community, she was the scapegoat. Not only had she followed a superintendent who was a legend, but when she demonstrated competency at doing what she was asked to do, she was referred to as too assertive and not feminine enough.

Similar to Eileen, she chose not to go public with some of these comments for fear that she would never get another superintendency. Some comments did make it to the newspaper and hurt her chances for another superintendency in the region. She is currently working through the disappointment and hurt as she pursues other searches. Because she is place-bound due to her family, she is taking interim positions at the building level or other central office positions.

Some domains that superintendents feel their evaluations should be based upon include the following (Glass & Franceschini, 2007):

1. Lead and manage personnel effectively   95.4%
2. Manage finances effectively   96.1%
3. Manage administrative functions effectively   91.2%
4. Foster effective school-community relations   94.3%
5. Have effective relationship with the board   90.0%
6. Foster a positive school climate   94.2%
7. Support and foster instruction   93.7%
8. Respect diversity and promote equality of opportunity   80.5%

Given the difficulty for women and persons of color attaining the position of superintendent, it was disheartening to note on the last item the much lower percentage of superintendents who believe their evaluations should include the domains of respect for diversity and promotion of equality of opportunity.

Superintendents are in a position of influence to create these opportunities for students, staff, administrators, and future superintendents. Janet wondered if she was not doing this in the position, who was? How is she a role model for the rest of her district? She wants all stakeholders to see that she values and promotes inclusion and opportunities for all.

Janet did admit that since NCLB she is very focused on this federal mandate in addition to the critical importance of the financial and political aspects of the position. However, sometimes she has to focus on her goals and the kids, otherwise all of this takes her away from the reason she got into the superintendency in the first place.

IN A NUTSHELL

- Keep close tabs on *the fit* and check with a variety of stakeholders to make sure this is intact. Be visible and observe with an eye toward what each group expects and perceives about your performance.
- Align your evaluation with goals that are congruent with your vision.
- Communicate frequently with the board and all stakeholders.
- Superintendents are in key positions to support diversity, equity, and inclusion in their districts.
- Know the criteria and process for how you will be evaluated. Keep documentation and copies of written evaluations for future use.

DEVELOPING PRESENCE

When Eileen enters the room, everyone notices. She has a presence that says, "I'm *here!*" When Annabelle enters the room, she also has a sense of presence—that whispers, "I'm here." Both are powerful and represent a very strong "I" but are very different.

Presence is the ability to remain authentic amid the chaos. Superintendents lead within systems. Some have greater chaos than others. Superintendents with presence understand that systems are self-renewing (Wheatley, 1992) and their interactions with these systems have far-reaching effects. Therefore, superintendents need to be reflective about how their actions occur. Their presence will enable them to navigate many changes and simultaneously lead others through these chaotic events. Whether it's a quiet or forceful presence, effective superintendents command presence as leaders (Richards, 2004).

What were some of the characteristics noted in the presence of many superintendents? Here are eleven of the traits (Gettle, 2004):

1. Very Positive Outlook

Juanita looks at everything with the glass at least half full, possibly up to the brim, despite many issues and blockers she encounters on a daily basis. She is able to talk positively about and bring out the best in her stakeholders, even those whom she considers detractors. She always tries to learn from those who were not her fans. She celebrates the successes of others rather than being threatened by their accomplishments.

2. Strong Sense of Self

Monique sent out energy that said, "I am worth it." She knows she is there for people, but she is also there for herself. By doing this she doesn't get eaten alive by those who do not support her. She thinks it might sound a little selfish, but she works hard at making sure this superintendency is meeting her needs.

By having her own needs met, Monique can then better meet the needs of others. It is like the announcement on the airplane that asks for you to put on your own air mask first before attempting to help others. It gives you more strength for the long term. She has boundaries and those around her know them. She is self-representative. However, there are those whose ego needs are so extreme that they exude more than presence; they exude narcissism. In one instance, Clare's predecessor was able to thrive on this type of behavior. However, when Clare tried to be self-representative, she was viewed as too unfeminine and her attempts at exuding presence were thwarted.

3. Control of the Emotions and Temperance

Betty also has a strong projected sense of self. She added that she needed to keep her emotions in check at all times. There is still some stereotyping that women are more emotional and thus cannot make the hard decisions. To counteract this, she is warm and friendly, but controlled. No one but those closest to her in her professional network, family, and friends see the manifestations of her emotions.

She especially keeps her anger and irritability in check. This does not mean that those around her do not know when she is angry about something. However, she controls how she expresses this anger and to whom. She is also controlled in her use of alcohol and in her relationships. Recently divorced, Betty is beginning to date. She is very careful to have her dates occur out of her district. She limits any alcohol consumption and rarely has a drink in any professional arena.

4. Excellent Communication Skills

The majority of the message individuals convey is done through non-verbal communication. How you stand and use your hands sends the real message of what you are trying to say. Maintaining eye contact in white Western culture is appropriate and adds to a sense of presence. However, those with presence are often aware of cultural differences related to eye contact, physical contact, and gestures. Eleanor talked about her handshake. She makes sure it is firm yet warm. If there is an attempt by a person in power to turn her hand upside down and assume more of a position of power, she gently turns her hand so they are shaking on an even playing field. She was equally aware that with some parents in her district who recently moved in from Korea, this may not be appropriate and would make them feel uncomfortable.

She is careful to ensure that all correspondence, whether to the board, the staff, her community, or her colleagues is error free. She knows that what she says is important, but how she says it sends a stronger message.

She is straightforward and sincere in her communication. She says what she means and means what she says.

By matching others' communicating styles, her message is much better heard. She tries to select the best words in any given situation knowing that language is an important factor in what others may hear. Under no circumstances does she use profanity in a professional situation.

Style and manner of speaking varied greatly among superintendents, but they all honed a style that worked for them. Each style of communicating needs to be very authentic for each superintendent. Eleanor is persuasive when necessary but keeps her voice pleasing and inviting. She is able to make dynamic presentations to a variety of stakeholder groups. She is compelling in her ability to engage others in these presentations and in dialogue with her. Demonstrating excellent communication skills is often an attribute of the superintendent that the board and stakeholders include when writing the vacancy profile for the recruitment brochure.

5. Awareness

Jane is known for her presence. When she arrives at a meeting she is warmly greeted by her colleagues. She remembers that Bill's wife just had surgery and asks about her well-being. She comments on a new colleague's hairstyle. She remembers Fred's birthday with a humorous card. She is attuned to those around her and everyone feels as though they are her best friend. She has the capacity to understand others' needs quickly and expresses concern for the issues they consider important. She is able to go beyond herself and celebrate the successes of all stakeholders.

She is aware of the different demands and needs of her staff at various ages and stages within their careers. She approaches individuals differently depending on this data. She knows that one teacher may need to be given a year off from committees because she is dealing with teenagers and aging parents simultaneously. She encourages a principal to suggest holding team meetings during lunch times, with teacher approval, so a young second-grade team member can get home at the end of the day to young children. She is visible within the schools and within the community. This attribute of visibility is one that also appears often on superintendent vacancy brochures.

6. Appearance

This doesn't mean that you are dressed to the nines; it means that your appearance matches your setting. Frances remembers asking what to wear for her interview. From one search consultant she was instructed to wear the traditional blue suit. She did, and when she got the job the board president told her that now that she had the job she might want to consider wearing something softer so she wouldn't intimidate the predominately farming community.

She struggled to decide if she was facing a potential Title IX issue or if this farmer was telling her something she really needed to hear. She let it play out and realized he was looking out for her best interest. She now wears a combination of attire that matches the situation, but she always looks professional. She tries to select clothes she likes and that fit her well so they contribute to her sense of well-being, especially on those days with long evening board meetings.

Appearance also means wearing a smile. It takes 12 muscles to smile and 103 to frown. Unless your face needs an aerobic workout, it is much easier to smile. Smiling also releases endorphins. Thus, you feel better and so does everyone else.

7. Tolerance and a Strong Sense of Social Justice

Diane assumed a superintendency in a community that has a burgeoning population of military families due to increased deployments from a nearby military base. She is working every day to model not only tolerance for the diversity this change brings to her district but also an embracing of the cultural capital these new students and families exemplify. She is helping teachers and administrators understand their filters for how they view these newcomers while owning her filters and the ways in which they color her decision making. She challenges these filters on a daily basis so she can make the most equitable decisions possible.

She is demonstrating problem-solving skills for meeting the needs of diverse learners while staying within the budget. She makes these decisions with input from others but makes necessary decisions efficiently. She demonstrates respect for everyone. Diane is viewing herself as a leader for social justice in her district and the community. She carries this aspect of her presence when she is a guest speaker at a local civic organization or during a weekly coffee hour with parents and community members. She strives to *be* the change she seeks.

8. Self-Motivated Goal Setter and Dreamer

Marcia is self-motivated. She always has been and attributes her success as a superintendent to this attribute. She knows how to set personal goals based on the vision and dreams she has for all students. She knows that to actualize her district's goals she needs buy-in from all stakeholders. Rather than trying to motivate others, which at times feels a bit more like manipulation, she chooses to envision her influence as empowering others. If she empowers them, the players and the changes will remain enhanced if she leaves the district to follow her own dreams.

She wants to leave everyone with a sense of hope that they can make whatever decisions and changes are necessary to meet the needs of a diverse student body. She wants everyone to have the opportunity to use their creativity every day to reach these goals so they are fulfilled and they fulfill others.

9. Sense of Humor

Allison, now at age fifty-four, believes that if she can't laugh while she's doing it, she's not going to do it. She knows that this does not mean laughter at the many serious moments and decisions that need to be made as superintendent. She does know this means that she can inject or appreciate laughter during 90 percent of her day when she is interacting with others in person, on the phone, or on e-mail. She knows her humor only includes that which does not reflect cultural stereotypes. She is very careful about the jokes she will repeat and knows that many educators have found themselves in awkward situations when they have forwarded a joke on e-mail that may not have been a prudent choice.

She can be self-deprecating and enjoys good-natured bantering. She is also keenly aware that sarcasm plays no role in her interactions. Sarcasm is not a sign of a sense of humor but rather is sophisticated bullying. When someone is the brunt of sarcasm she or he has no choice but to laugh, lest they look like a killjoy. The laughing is merely to save face. Sarcasm might be used between personal friends but never when a power differential is extant. The subordinate again will have no choice but to laugh. What will appear as joint laughter at the moment may create more problems as the unequal relationship continues.

10. Humility

Above all, those with the strongest presence are humble. Their presence is a given and they don't need to keep reminding others of their importance or accomplishments. They just do what they do for a reason greater than themselves. This unselfish leading gives them purpose, which gives them the presence to bring others along with their vision. They keep their egos in check and are grateful for the opportunities they have been given to make a true difference for children and families. The accolades they receive are nice to hear but the true accolades come from within. Leading with a higher aim will be discussed further in chapter 4.

11. So, What Is Missing?

Many of us hate odd numbers. Would you rather this list had been ten or twelve items? Some of us like tidy lists and predictable frameworks. But a key piece for those with presence is the tolerance for ambiguity and their ability to be flexible. They can navigate within chaos to reach their goals.

Joanne tells a story of having to balance many stakeholders' opinions and perspectives when crafting the best possible new building configuration and ensuing capital project. She had to be flexible and keep everyone moving forward through a process that seemed like architectural molasses. She had a presence that manifested itself a bit differently in each situation, but she was who she was. It was because of that stable presence that the project came to fruition and was successful. She could *tolerate ambiguity.* She had to get used to all the "elevens" that would be part of her superintendency.

This presence comes from a sense of passion about what one does (Bolman & Deal, 2006). Confidence can be developed (Bixler & Dugan, 1997), but presence must come from within. This sense of presence needs to have consistent attention and one must be true to one's authentic self in the process. It is important for successful superintendents to find their sense of self that is present during calm times and crisis.

In their book *Presence*, Senge, Scharmer, Jaworski, and Flowers (2004) talk about additional elements of presence that characterize leading with higher aims. Jaworski (1996) also describes how synchronicity plays a role in one's ability to respond that may lead to becoming a leader with a greater sense of a higher aim. Their thoughts link to that concept and will be shared in chapter 4 in this book.

IN A NUTSHELL

When developing a sense of presence, superintendents might want to assess how they view themselves relative to the following:

- A very positive outlook
- A strong sense of self
- Control of the emotions and temperance
- Excellent communication skills—verbal, nonverbal, and written
- Awareness of others
- Professional appearance that matches the district
- Tolerance and a strong sense of social justice
- A self-motivated goal setter and dreamer
- A sense of humor
- Humility
- Tolerance for ambiguity
- Consistency during times of calm and crisis
- Knowledge of systems within schools, the self-organizing principles by which change occurs in organizations, and the role of facilitators of that change

STAYING CURRENT

The state organization for all superintendents regularly held professional development opportunities for Olivia and other new school chiefs. Topics for discussion and study included, but were not limited to, superintendent-school board relationships, school budget management, working collaboratively with local and state political leaders, and legal matters of importance. These training sessions were oftentimes held regionally, due to the high number of retiring superintendents leading to the hiring of numerous new ones. Instructors for the in-service training were experienced superintendents noted for their expertise in a particular area of significance. These statewide professional organizations, whose names and addresses are listed in appendix C in the back of this book, helped increase Olivia's learning and kept her current.

Olivia also made it a practice to read professional journals, bulletins, newsletters, and new legislative information on a regular basis. Part of the balance in her life was achieved by planning to set aside time each day to read these job-related materials. Though oftentimes difficult, if not impossible, she strived to do this to keep her knowledge and leadership skills fresh.

Regional educational centers, local law firms, and colleges and universities offered formal coursework and/or seminars for Olivia and her colleagues. As the leaders in school districts, superintendents must stay abreast of any legal or regulatory changes at the federal and state levels.

These seminars, workshops, and classes were often great opportunities for Olivia to network. While doing this, she could ascertain who among her colleagues had greater knowledge, more refined skills, and better experiences in areas where Olivia was weak. Colleagues could share and help each other. The camaraderie in the group was strong and potent. Supportive colleagues, who were all in the same spotlight in their school communities' collective eyes, surrounded Olivia. Colleagues kept each other current and supported each other. This was truly a win-win situation for Olivia and all the other school district leaders.

Superintendents must keep up with all the many changes that happen frequently. In addition to dealing with the everyday minutia of the job and the all too frequently unexpected occurrences in the district, superintendents should avail themselves, whenever possible, of the different opportunities that exist for staying current in the knowledge, skills, and dispositions they need for the top school leadership position.

Nearly every state in the union has a centralized professional organization for superintendents. These organizations provide a wide range of professional development opportunities (Tucker, 2002). State organizations, their local branches, and the national organization for superintendents—American Association for School Administrators (AASA)—focus their efforts on developing, motivating, teaching, and supporting superintendents. The mission of AASA is "to support and develop effective school system leaders who are dedicated to the highest quality public education for all children" (AASA, 2006, p. i).

A superintendent's workday is long, to say the least. Within those work hours, superintendents should attempt to set aside time, each day preferably, to *read professional materials* that come into the office. Online information is readily available also. Though carving out professional reading time during the workday is next to impossible, it is imperative that superintendents read to remain current in the field. Superintendents should design their own schedule, be it during the workweek or on the weekends, for professional reading and stick to the schedule whenever possible.

Superintendents' time is often not their own. However, signing up for a college course may be the way to help a superintendent stay current. Superintendent contracts often contain monetary provisions for advanced study. If a superintendent registers for a course that meets on a certain night at specific times, then perhaps that will allow the superintendent who does this a convenient way to stay on top of new developments in the field. Making that commitment to coursework might just be the reason a superintendent stays current in the job.

Still, *no other source of support and staying current is better than one's colleagues.* Superintendents each have their own areas of knowledge, skills, and expertise. Colleagues are usually more than willing to share and assist (Grogan & Brunner, 2005). There exists a great bond between school chiefs. No one of them is an island, and not one stands alone for very long. Superintendents are very skilled at helping keep each other on their individual and collective toes.

IN A NUTSHELL

- Statewide professional organizations exist that serve as learning and support centers for superintendents. Please see appendix C of this book for contact information for these organizations.
- Superintendents should set aside, as often as possible, reading time for job-related materials.
- Colleges and universities may be good sources of professional development for superintendents.
- Superintendents should seek each other's assistance in their attempt to stay current in the position.
- Online resources may be very helpful here also.

ACHIEVING PERSONAL BALANCE

Personal balance is different for everyone, as these individual stories will illustrate. In her early efforts seeking a superintendency and confident that she would do a good job, Nicole knew that she had to address both professional issues and personal ones. Prior to applying for a certain superintendency, she drove to the school district and asked herself, point blank, if she could live there and have a personal life. Nicole ate at local restaurants, spent the night in the community, and perused the local newspaper. She struck up general conversations with the people she met. In the process of determining if this position would be a match for her professionally, she also found that a personal life in the school district community would indeed be possible. Nicole struck a balance.

Susan had grown up in the area where she was superintendent, though she had previously worked in different school leadership positions in other areas of the state. As a child in this area, she had shown horses as part of her 4H Club experiences. The geography of the area, with its rolling hills and the four seasons of weather for outdoor activities, suited her. Susan knew that she would need to make time to play as often as she could. She vowed to take the time for herself, and she did.

Tess exclaimed that she must be nuts when asked why she was a superintendent. But, she realized that, in order to be a successful superintendent, she would have to balance work and family. Oftentimes working seventy or more hours per week, she focused on the quality of family time together, particularly during the very busy parts of the school year.

Ruby, whose two children were students in the school district she led, maintained her life balance by segmenting work and home as much as she possibly could. She focused on the job Monday through Friday, which worked fairly well while her children were in high school. Ruby attended school functions at night, often those in which her children participated (athletics, music, dances). Saving Saturdays and Sundays for her personal life, she often retreated to a family home in another part of the state for rest, relaxation, and reconnecting with family members and friends. This she has practiced throughout her tenure as a superintendent.

Kathleen offers some advice for your personal self—take your vacations and keep your personal life intact. Like most administrators, in her early years, Kathleen was scared to death to leave the office. What if something happened while she was not there? Of course the district had managed to survive without her being there for the previous sixty-plus years, but that did not matter. Kathleen needed to be at her watch 24/7. She accumulated scads of vacation time for which that she will never get compensated. Eventually she became uncomfortable about even the notion of taking a vacation.

Finally, in a bold move, Kathleen took off both a Friday and a Monday (of course, no students or faculty were in school on those days). In the afternoon on Saturday, while happily performing the mundane task of mowing a large lawn, she realized that she was not thinking about school problems. While lounging on the deck looking at the lake, Kathleen realized that she was reflecting about where she thought the next steps should be for the district. She wrote down some notes and closed the book. By midday Sunday, she was able to read a book for pleasure. She was becoming more productive about her thoughts on the district and was able to balance things she liked to do for pleasure with things she liked and needed to think about for work.

This is not any revelation. It is commonly known that one can be more productive when not working all of the time. However, Kathleen found that her colleagues, who were mostly men, were better able to achieve that balance, and she wondered why.

When taking on the role of superintendent, many like Kathleen did not relinquish any of their duties as wife, partner, daughter, caregiver, or mother. Kathleen still mowed the lawn, performed snow removal, did laundry (yes, even hanging clothes on the clothesline), shopped for weekly groceries, cleaned, made sure the holiday decorations were up and then taken down and packed away, prepared meals when coming together as a family, and did any other domestic task that needed to be done. Most of these duties are not universally shared equally or equitably in a household, so Kathleen did not think that she was unique.

Of the aforementioned duties, the lawn mowing and snow removal, traditionally held as male duties in the household, could easily be subbed and, as she later found out, were in fact subbed out by many of her male colleagues. But, that still left everything else.

The point of the story is simple—take vacation time. Additionally, before getting into the lifestyle of the superintendency, be very purposeful in thinking through those chores at home that you simply will not have time to attend to in the same manner as pre-superintendency. These are points to be well taken by all school superintendents.

When someone takes on the role of superintendent, he or she is embarking on a lifestyle change. This change will include one's entire household, and no one should kid themselves that it will not. The days when it was appropriate to go to the grocery store in a pair of cut-offs, T-shirt, and flip-flops or sweats and sneakers will be a distant memory. Everyone will see the superintendent's published salary. With the superintendent's face in the school newsletter or in the local press for some event or another story, someone will recognize her or him and wonder why this public figure is not dressed professionally on that Wednesday night or Saturday afternoon—after all, look at the salary they pay the superintendent. In other words, the right to privacy is gone.

Going out to dinner? Picking up a bottle of wine in the liquor store? Worse yet, what car does the superintendent drive to work? All is fair game and ripe for discussion among school district residents.

Try explaining that to teenagers. A superintendent's children may have a difficult time understanding that their actions are being reviewed as well as their mother's, but under a much different microscope than before. "It's not fair," they may lament. No, it is not, but the role of superintendent requires a lifestyle change.

Superintendents represent everyone in the school community. Whether on the clock or off, the superintendent is still the superintendent. Kathleen is a wife, mother, daughter, and superintendent. It is a balancing act that requires tweaking all of the time. In her district, she purposefully invites her husband to specific school events to remind the district residents that she is a wife and mother as well as their superintendent. She is a woman who is capable of being a formidable figure and yet still being feminine. Others might involve their spouses, partners, or children in a different way, but it needs to be agreed upon by the family members so everyone feels as comfortable as possible.

On a side note, Kathleen stopped inviting her children to district events. After luring one of them out with the promise of gas money, she saw his anguished look as he endured the fifth-grade band concert. She duly noted the copy of the Geneva Conference rules regarding torture that was placed on her computer the next morning. She got the message, loud and clear.

All of this is just words. Kathleen has lived these words, but she knows that if someone said all of this to her she would have still moved ahead and not really put any credence in this. She would have rationalized that her house was in order.

Achieving personal balance for those women in the top school leadership positions involves *both personal and professional considerations* (Williamson & Hudson, 2003). This is sometimes hard to achieve, but a successful superintendency warrants it. While the superintendency most likely will be professionally challenging most of the time, the personal considerations involve issues with self, family, and friends. It is a balancing act, one that must be addressed and worked on practically all the time (Houston, 2001).

Many successful female superintendents begin the journey to establish that personal balance well before the first day of work. Their personal life has to be a match with a district at least as much as the professional fit. Superintendents speak about the need to find happiness in the position (Williamson & Hudson, 2003). The superintendency is too difficult a job on any given day to not enjoy the position and love the work that you do. The fit is critical to a superintendent's success.

The acts of going home or returning to one's roots sometimes help superintendents with the balance between work and family. Going home may mean a return to a place where everybody knows your name. Friends from long ago may still be there and can serve as extra pairs of eyes and ears in the community. Family may also still live in the school district. Between family and friends a support system exists which will only benefit a superintendent in his/her work (Grogan & Brunner, 2005).

One way that some superintendents successfully balance work and family is to focus on the *quality of time spent with family and friends.* Long hours are a staple of the superintendency. Public scrutiny is also a reality for a superintendent. This affects a superintendent's personal life. Spouses and/or significant others must be counted on for support. Children, particularly if they attend school in the district in which the parent is the superintendent, are vulnerable to public opinion and as much scrutiny or more as the superintendent herself. While the superintendent may not spend as much time with family and friends due to the time demands of the job, the focus should be on the quality of the time together. Oftentimes, that is all one gets.

If time spent in the professional role can be segmented from time spent in the family mode, then this is another way of dealing with achieving personal balance in the life of a school superintendent. Many superintendents do not divide their lives this way. Those who are able to do this strongly believe that this is a viable way to strike that balance between work and play. Personal time is coveted and highly protected, for obvious reasons. Whatever ways superintendents are able to steal time for the personal portion of their lives will directly impact the success of their superintendency.

IN A NUTSHELL

- Achieving balance in one's life involves issues both professional and personal in nature.

- Applicants for the superintendency should test the waters beforehand to determine if a personal life is congruent with the school leadership position being sought.
- Sometimes *going home*, wherever that is and whatever it entails, is key to establishing a workable professional and personal life.
- Superintendents oftentimes focus on the *quality* of family time spent together, versus the *quantity* of time taken up by the position.
- Segmenting the week into work-related activities from Monday through Friday and family and friend–related activities reserved for the weekends is one way some school leaders achieve personal balance in their lives.
- Superintendents should remember to take care of themselves, as well as family and the school district community.

LEADING WITH A HIGHER AIM

It looked doubtful that Jill's district's budget would pass; the board president was leading a tax pact group and not only welcomed but also cheered and jeered along with resistors who were present at every board meeting. This board member also began an online chat room where he voiced his concerns about the capability of the superintendent, the greediness of the teachers, and overall discontent in the school district. But when he began sharing information that had been discussed in executive sessions, it was time to get the state commissioner involved. The school board president had truly crossed the line.

Jill still hung in there and did not give up. She didn't let these obstacles blur her vision for the district, at least she didn't let on that her confidence was faltering. She was acting in an ethical manner and knew she could look at herself in the mirror at night—and that the board president could not. She was leading with a higher aim—for a reason better, larger, or stronger than what is readily apparent. She knew there might be material goods (i.e., tax dollars) that could not simultaneously belong to both taxpayers and the district. But, some nonmaterial goods (e.g., respect) that represented leading with a higher aim, could.

During a writing project initiated by superintendent Darcy and nine of her veteran teachers, such leadership was evident. The writing team's purpose was to learn what kept these twenty-five-plus-year veteran teachers still vibrant as educators. The teachers and superintendent all met on their own time on Saturdays to write, share, and edit. Darcy participated along with her teachers and was keenly interested in what kept them striving and thriving when many others, with a similar number of years of teaching, had settled down for a long winter's nap. Through their stories and reflections, STARS: **S**ervice, **T**alents, a higher **A**im, **R**eflection, and **S**upport was founded.

So what does this initiative have to do with the superintendents we have learned about in this book? Similar to these superintendents, these teachers began their careers because they had a strong desire to serve (S). They were able to use their individual talents every day (T). These talents were valued and strengthened. They engaged in reflection (R). They reflected on their practice and found ways for mutual needs to be met—their own personal growth as well as that of the students within a learning community. Finally, if support (S) was evident from building and district leadership, their practice was enhanced. But they didn't let lack of support deter them. They were going to be intrinsically motivated whether their teaching was outwardly supported and valued or not.

The teachers served students according to a higher aim (A). Their responses centered around their knowledge that they had a bigger purpose and wanted to make a difference. For some, this was talked about within a spiritual dimension. For others, it was within a social justice context; they wanted to give students equity in their educational experiences and opportunities; they wanted the next generation to have more access to learning in an environment that was safe from harm, bullying, and abuse. They wanted to right wrongs that were done to them as children and break cultural barriers and stereotypes. They wanted cultural proficiency reflected in their settings. Some talked passionately about wanting equity for all and inclusion of all students.

Similar higher aims drive the work of superintendents. Why do they do this job when sometimes it seems so enervating or hopeless? What keeps them going? What is their bigger purpose? Why did they get into it in the first place? The superintendents wanted to have more power to make a difference for more children. They wanted to do a better job than those who previously led their districts. They wanted to not be the type of leader they have complained about in the past.

Some came to their districts having grown up in families where education was valued. Others came as first-generation children to finish high school or to go to college. Some had a strong faith in a higher power; some had a strong faith in humankind. Some fell into their roles more easily than others, but now all were in a position of power. Did they view this position as having some level of privilege that they could use to their advantage? Were they able to recognize this privilege, whether it be race, economic standing, or access? Were they able to apply it to embrace the diversity in their districts?

Those who led with a higher aim in mind were able to look at the diversity and cultural capital their students and staff brought to school as assets, not liabilities. This cultural capital might be race, gender, ethnicity, social class, ability, sexual orientation, or other ways of defining individuals or groups who have traditionally been viewed negatively.

LEADERSHIP AND SOCIAL JUSTICE

Leadership and social justice have a strong relationship (Larson & Murtadha, 2002; Larson & Ovando, 2001; Owens & Ovando, 2000; Skrla, Reyes, & Scheurich, 2000). Those with a strong sense of social justice led with higher aims. It was that strong sense of social justice that was paramount in Tanya's decision-making process.

Tanya's district has had increasing enrollment due to the enlargement of an army base because of increased deployments to the war. Many of the students were adding diverse cultural capital to schools, especially related to race and poverty. Tanya and other leaders in the region were asked if the diversity that these new students brought was viewed as cultural capital to build on or an annoyance to try and get rid of somehow. As you might guess, there was a range of responses, but the dialogue that occurred was a very powerful one. It needed to take place. They needed to discuss the *elephant in the room*. It was risky for those involved in the dialogue, but it was more risky to pretend it didn't exist and then try to educate these students with so much going unsaid.

The sense of social justice expressed by superintendents involves a focus on not just teaching and learning but also meeting the needs of every child, every day; it also involves a proactive system of support and inclusive structures (Bogotch, 2002; Frattura & Capper, 2007).

Some of the superintendents engaged in dialogues about this diversity that reflected a particular code of ethics. The American Association of School Administrators (AASA, 2008) developed a code of ethics that is in appendix B of this book. Wilmore (2008) provides a very clear link between the Educational Leadership Constituent Council's (ELCC) standard 5 on ethical behavior and practice of a superintendent. Similar practices are evident in the personal code of ethics of those who lead with higher aims.

INTENTIONAL BEHAVIOR

Leaders are to practice and serve in ways that cultivate awareness, empathy, and wisdom. These leaders are good listeners and as Covey (2004) states in his first "seven habits," seek first to understand rather than be understood. He also suggests that leaders recognize their eighth spiritual habit. These leaders listen to all stakeholders, not just those who agree with their positions.

Tanya listened to the teachers who felt overburdened with more students now identified as having special needs. She listened to principals who were spending more of their day on issues related to family support and classroom management.

Leadership practices are to be designed and conducted in ways that respect the common good, with due regard for safety, health, and order. Because the increased awareness gained from practices can catalyze desire for personal and social change, leaders need to use special care to help direct the energies of those they serve, as well as the actions based on their own perspectives, in responsible ways that reflect a regard for all.

Tanya had to weigh what was good for the largest group of students rather than a core of students who had received additional opportunities in the past. These decisions were riddled with past history and priorities, politics, and publicity. She had to hold firm to what she knew was right. And she was so grateful that she had just negotiated her own new three-year contract.

Leaders respect and seek to preserve the autonomy and dignity of each stakeholder. Leaders make reasonable preparations to protect each participant's health and safety during times of change and in the periods of vulnerability that may follow. They are resilient and keep going when times are difficult (Reed & Patterson, 2007).

When an irate parent came into Tanya's office because her son was not allowed to come to school for joking about having a knife, Tanya listened with empathy but held firm that her job was to protect the safety of all students, even if the parent were a board member.

Leaders assist with only those skills for which they are qualified by personal experience, by training, or by education. By continually updating these skills, they are stronger leaders. They utilize a collaborative approach to problem solving that includes expertise and skills from a wide network of stakeholders.

Tanya engaged in ongoing professional development for herself in areas related to finance, law, public relations, media relations, boardsmanship, legislative issues, and new trends in curriculum and instruction. She attended some of this professional development with her leadership team and some with the entire staff. She then used a shared decision-making forum to design, implement, and evaluate the professional development opportunities for the district.

Effective leaders solicit feedback from other leaders to help ensure the integrity of their practices. They are continually adding to the context of what is meant by social justice (Furman & Gruenewald, 2004). Tanya knew she was held to a higher standard than most in her community. Implicit in her role was also the notion of being a moral leader. She's careful about where she socializes, the roles she and her family play in the community, and how she will choose to be visible. She is expected to be exceptionally ethical and to make ethical decisions at all times.

Tanya didn't believe in motivating others. She saw that as manipulative. Instead she presented alternatives and found ways for staff members to develop their own passion for different aspects of student learning. She had absolutes that were nonnegotiable but knew that if changes were going to last well after she had left the district, they must come from within her staff members.

Senge et al. (2004) embellish on leading with a higher aim through a sense of presence. Consistent with the work of Wheatley (1992) which was described earlier in this book, they suggest aspects that they would ask the reader to consider, including the following:

- A leader's presence is connected with the self-organizing system of a living institution. The school organization will evolve toward this vision of a higher aim given time, support, and the right culture and climate.
- Deeper levels of learning are noted in those with presence.
- Those with presence are fully conscious and live in the present moment.
- They are deep listeners.
- Those with presence are able to go beyond one's preconceptions and usual ways of making sense and making decisions.
- They are able to let go of old identities and their need to control.
- They not only let go, but also *let come* as they participate in the larger field for change.
- They demonstrate the capacity to suspend judgment and the need to direct or control.
- They have the courage to *see freshly*.
- They are able to see the whole coming from within the organization. They also recognize the work of redirecting to achieve this wholeness.
- They surrender into *commitment* and seek emerging understanding.
- They deal with fragmentation with an eye to the whole as they help themselves and others rediscover purpose.
- They are able to notice and act on moments of synchronicity—those events that occur simultaneously with a deep underlying connection if one is able to see.

Effective leaders practice openness and respect toward people whose beliefs are in apparent contradiction to their own. They are inclusive of others regardless of their race, gender, socioeconomic standing, sexual preference, culture, or other variables.

Tanya understands the difficulty of working with a diverse group of faculty and staff. There are myriad benefits but also there are skills, content, and dispositions that are necessary so everyone can understand one another and value differences. This is an ongoing process that needs daily attention.

Leaders strive to be aware of how their own belief systems, values, needs, and limitations affect their work. There isn't a night that goes by that Tanya doesn't look in the mirror and ask herself if she made the best decisions possible that day. She looks out the window for her vision but in the mirror for her reflection. Could she live with herself given the decisions she made that day?

One superintendent, who is also an adjunct professor in a preparation program for emerging leaders, worked with her colleague to create the *Guilly Rubric for Ethical Decision Making* (Gilmour & Tingley, 2001). Leaders use this rubric to help them make decisions that are congruent with their leading with a higher aim. These decisions are made in the best interests of all persons of diversity for the greater good. A portion of the rubric is included in this chapter.

Tanya used this rubric in table 4.1 almost unconsciously sometimes while making decisions. At other times she consciously went through all the steps and remembered to gather as much data as possible before making a decision. This data also included her own intuition and inner knowledge regarding what was most ethical in the situation.

Furman and Sheilds (2003) described one woman in their study, Delia, who was a new African American superintendent. Her definition of social justice mirrored many of the attributes described on the Guilly Rubric. Delia has a strong desire to be fair to all concerned, to be reflective, and to be equitable to all.

Furman and Sheilds (2003) categorized their findings related to how superintendents support and promote social justice in their settings. How do these apply to you? You may want to use the chart in table 4.2 to record your personal thoughts and reflections.

Betty indicated that her reason for leading with a higher aim was to uphold the value of public education. Marcia believed that students need to see women in positions of authority and they need to see women as role models with integrity. Frances knew for herself that she needed to be publicly accountable for ensuring that each child had the best education possible. Allison did what she did because she believed that we need to continue our society in a way that is equitable for all.

Table 4.1. Guilly Rubric for Ethical Decision Making

Elements in the Ethical Decision-Making Process	4 (Exemplary)	3 (Proficient)
Values and beliefs that are in conflict in this dilemma	The decision maker is very clear about what values and beliefs are in conflict. The decision maker can list most of them.	The decision maker is clear about what values and beliefs are in conflict. The decision maker can list many of them.
The individuals who are affected by the decision	The decision maker is very clear about who will be affected by the decision. The decision maker can name them.	The decision maker is clear about who will be affected by the decision. The decision maker can name them.
What is best for the individuals involved	The decision maker is clear about how the decision is being made in the best interest of all those involved. She or he can describe to others how this determination was reached.	The decision maker is mostly clear about how the decision is being made in the best interest of all those involved. She or he can describe in some detail to others how this determination was reached.
What is best for the institution	The decision maker is clear about how the decision is being made in the best interest of the institution. She or he can describe to others how this determination was reached.	The decision maker is clear about how the decision is being made in the best interest of the institution. She or he can describe in some detail to others how this determination was reached.

Criteria		
The possible effects for the decision maker himself or herself	The decision maker is very clear about the ramifications of the decision for himself or herself personally and professionally. She or he can articulate most of the consequences and accepts these.	The decision maker is clear about the ramifications of the decision for himself or herself personally and professionally. She or he can articulate some of the consequences and accepts these.
The future ramifications of this decision	The decision maker can describe possible future ramifications of this decision. It is clear that he or she has thought about and planned for these future ramifications.	The decision maker can describe some possible future ramifications of this decision. It is clear that he or she has thought about and planned for most of these future ramifications.
Legality of solution	The solution is clear-cut and legal.	The solution is somewhat clear-cut and legal.
Fairness of solution	The solution is fair to all persons involved.	The solution is fair to nearly all persons involved.
	All persons treated fairly can be identified.	Nearly all persons who receive fair treatment can be identified. Decision maker is aware of those not treated fairly.
Demonstration of respect and caring for all those involved by the decision maker	The decision maker demonstrates consistent caring and respect for all persons involved. Feedback from all stakeholders reflects this caring and respect.	The decision maker demonstrates consistent caring and respect for all persons involved. Feedback from most stakeholders reflects this caring and respect.

Table 4.2. Dimensions of Leadership

Dimension of Leadership	Awareness of Key Issues	Your Personal Evidence
1. Ethical and moral	Values of the community; Discussables and non-discussables (Barth, 2004)	
2. Communal and Contextual	Socio/cultural/economic community of the school; Traditions; Patterns of interaction?	
3. Processual	Opportunities for inquiry, decision making; Who is privileged or marginalized in decision making or dialogue?	
4. Transformative	What changes have been introduced? What does critique look like in the community?	
5. Pedagogical	What about the formal curriculum? The informal curriculum? The written vs. taught curriculum? Values and beliefs? Assessments? Who succeeds?	

Barbara was a foster parent and was a single foster parent for quite a while. She knew that the community must all work together to help raise all their children. In her position as superintendent she has been able to provide more opportunities for all children within her district. She was working to create healthy schools that foster equity while including individual growth for all students and staff. She wanted staff to be comfortable with ambiguity while all the pieces got put into place.

Clare wanted her leadership to bring back the absolute joy of learning. She recognized the need for accountability but wanted to create lifelong learners who are intrinsically motivated and curious. JoAnne believed in shared decision making but believed the vision must be set and articulated at the top—where she thrives. Her own children had a wonderful experience in public schools and she wanted this for all children. She knew that many students do not have the support her own children had and she knew how critical that support was to their success. She led with a higher aim to encourage creative pathways to create this support.

Eileen led with a higher aim by creating high expectations for all students. She encouraged her staff and students to pursue postsecondary education at our nation's Ivy League universities. Many in her district believe that these students could aspire to that level of education. It is tough to break the stereotypes for students who can't seek more learning through higher education. To make this happen, issues of race and prejudice need to be faced head on. Dialogue about these issues should occur in every arena of our school communities.

As part of her focus on social justice, Eileen realized that she needed to lead her staff to a critical consciousness to prepare all students to live in today's society. Eileen herself had to hold a critical consciousness about power, privilege, and inequities in society and in her schools (McKensie, Christman, Hernandez, Fierro, Capper, Dantley, Gonzalez, Cambron-McCabe, & Scheurich, 2008). As the superintendent, Eileen knew it was her responsibility to start these conversations.

However, she stated that in her first two years she felt like an imposter in the job. She could barely do all the tasks required. Yet she knew she had to have a clear vision and tackle some of the roadblocks that were standing in the way of our children, especially those from poverty, who were not achieving. She believed it was her failures and life lessons that enabled her to have the greatest positive impact in the long run. She took a risk on the big pieces, but not taking those risks was not an option for her. It would have meant forgoing her purpose and she wouldn't have been able to live with that as her legacy.

Juanita knew that part of her leading with a higher aim was to create a leadership team that functioned very well together. This teamwork enabled many changes to occur that she would not have been able to do alone. She indicated that the job was a daunting one, and at times she never felt so disrespected, doubted, or lonely. As much as developing this team was her passion, she could not turn to them for her support. This was where her network became critical. She did, however, turn to her team for humor and laughter to help her get through the tough spots of leading with a higher aim.

Seeking to sustain superintendents in their current roles, despite the many challenges and often too little positive feedback, can be addressed by reflecting on some of the factors that brought them initially to education and leadership. Superintendents can reflect on the ways in which they lead with higher aims and share these with their colleagues and staff. Superintendents do make a marked difference on the lives of children, who will become the next generation of citizens and individuals who are capable of living lives that are filled with capacity, respect, success, and caring.

IN A NUTSHELL

- Leading a school district means leading with a higher aim.
- The leader's higher aim may be social justice, cultural proficiency, democratic community, spirituality, equity, or a personal wrong that needs to be righted.
- Keeping oneself and one's staff vibrant is characterized by STARS: Service is given to others; Talents are used every day; higher Aim leadership means leading for the bigger purpose; Reflection is inherent and is ongoing; and Support comes from others, is intrinsic, or both.

- Leading with a higher aim may be about intention, serving society, serving individuals, competence, integrity, quiet presence, tolerance, and peer review.
- Leading with a higher aim may be enhanced by using ethical decision-making tools such as ethical standards or the Guilly Rubric.
- Those who engage in leading with a higher aim have a presence that is characterized by letting go, letting come, the capacity to suspend, understanding of self-organizing systems, redirection of the organization from within, and synchronicity.

5

JOURNALING

Several superintendents interviewed for this book hinted at their personal practice of journaling or reflective writing. Vivian directly connected her periodic journaling to success in the superintendency. She firmly believes that those who are reflective (not reactive, but proactive) will be successful in school district leadership.

Many superintendents believe that keeping a journal is a key element for successful superintendents. Their belief is so strong that not only is journaling beneficial for them, but it also provides an excellent model for their leadership teams. As the school district superintendent, Kathleen requires that each of her building and district leaders keep a journal for reflection on their leadership experiences.

Why keep a journal? First of all, Kathleen realizes that she will easily forget. Superintendents move constantly from the macro to the micro and back again. They will be threatened in one second and hugged in another. It is so surreal and yet so very grounded and real. Similar to how Lyndon Johnson once described the presidency, being superintendent can be an "exquisite hell."

Jill joins Kathleen in suggesting that superintendents should take the time to record what they believe to be worthy of memorializing. Looking back, superintendents will be surprised at their accomplishments and how far they have grown. They will have forgotten what the crisis of the day was, but they will have kept it as a battle scar and not repeat it. It seems like one more thing to do at the time, but they will be better for the experience. Superintendents' handwriting or keyboarding will improve with this practice if nothing else.

Frances and Tanya know that by reflecting in their journal, they are at least taking a few moments in their day to calm down a bit and remember why they took the job in the first place. It's easy to focus on what else needs to be done rather than remembering all that has been accomplished, and hopefully accomplished better because of one's leadership.

Reflection is the art of self-talk, which helps those who practice it make sense of a situation, issue, or experience; evaluate their skills, actions, or reasoning; determine what worked or did not work; and decide what might need to happen in order to improve (Sergiovanni, 2008). It is a way to look at you and assess your own personal and professional knowledge, skills, and dispositions (Schon, 1983).

Journaling is the practice of recording those reflections. Oftentimes, the mere act of either handwriting or typing the reflections gives the school leader cause to step away from the daily turmoil of the job and think through what has occurred. It may work as good therapy for the bruised soul. Additionally, journaling can be used as a method of communication and discourse in mentoring new school superintendents (Hopkins-Thompson, 2000). If nothing else, it provides a concrete record of actions taken and decisions made.

Listed on the following pages are a variety of questions, similar to those asked of current, successful female superintendents in the research for this book. These questions will, hopefully, spark reflection on the part of aspiring superintendents. Space is provided after each question for readers to record their thoughts. Look at yourself, what you do, how you do it, and why you do what you do. What are your beliefs? It is all about the learning. And the first place to learn is you.

Journaling may provide a guide or map in your adventure into the superintendency. As stated in chapter 1, this practice may help you clarify your vision for the superintendency and craft an entry plan into this top school leadership position. We hope you have enjoyed the read, and we ask that you take some time to reflect. Please feel free to write until your heart is content. Remember, it is good for the soul, too.

REFLECTIVE QUESTIONS FOR ASPIRING SUPERINTENDENTS

Reflective Question #1: Why are you considering the superintendency?

_____
_____
_____
_____
_____

Reflective Question #2: What makes you stand out from other potential candidates for the superintendency?

_____
_____
_____
_____
_____

Reflective Question #3: What skills, dispositions, and personalities do you possess that would make you an attractive superintendent candidate to a district?

_____
_____
_____
_____
_____

Reflective Question #4: Do you have any role models and how do they influence you?

_____
_____
_____
_____
_____

Reflective Question #5: Have you been mentored? If so, from whom and what have you learned? Whom have you mentored?

_____

_____

_____

_____

_____

Reflective Question #6: What have you been doing throughout your professional life to enhance your candidacy for the superintendency?

_____

_____

_____

_____

_____

Reflective Question #7: While each superintendency has its own specific set of circumstances, what have you observed about who is successful and who is not in this job?

_____

_____

_____

_____

_____

Reflective Question #8: Why do you do what you do? How do you lead _a fortiori?_

_____

_____

_____

_____

Reflective Question #9: What can others learn from your successes?

_____

_____

_____

_____

_____

Reflective Question #10: Do you consider yourself a "Keeper of the Dream"? Why or why not?

_____

_____

_____

_____

_____

Appendix A

SUPERINTENDENT RESEARCH QUESTIONNAIRE

Superintendent Research [Fall 2005/Summer 2006]

Name _____ Date Interviewed _____

School District _____

Interview Questions for **Superintendents**:

1. Tell me about your career path to the superintendency.

_____

_____

_____

_____

_____

2. How many searches were you in prior to obtaining this position?

_____

_____

_____

_____

_____

3. What are your experiences in the superintendent search process?

_____

_____

_____

_____

_____

4. How did you prepare for your interviews?

_____

_____

_____

_____

_____

5. What made you stand out from the other candidates interviewed?

_____

_____

_____

_____

_____

6. What skills, dispositions, and personalities contributed to the school district hiring you?

_____

_____

_____

_____

_____

7. Why was this district a "match" for you?

_____

_____

_____

_____

_____

8. What behaviors of the search consultant were utilized to help you move forward in the search process?

_____

_____

_____

_____

_____

9. Did you have any role models and how did they influence you?

_____

_____

_____

_____

_____

10. What kind of mentoring, networking, and/or preparation did you experience for the superintendency?

_____

_____

_____

_____

_____

11. Can you talk to me about the process for negotiating your contract?

_____

_____

_____

_____

_____

12. Was the salary portion of your contract settled in the high end, low end, or middle range?

_____

_____

_____

_____

_____

13. What have you done to develop a positive relationship with your school board?

_____

_____

_____

_____

_____

14. Tips for sustaining that successful relationship between superintendent and BOE?

_____

_____

_____

_____

_____

15. How do you handle criticism from the board or from the community?

_____

_____

_____

_____

_____

16. How have you maneuvered the political waters of your school district?

_____

_____

_____

_____

_____

17. Tips for maneuvering the political waters of a school district?

_____

_____

_____

_____

_____

18. How have you successfully worked with the media?

_____

_____

_____

_____

_____

19. Tips for nurturing positive media relationships?

_____

_____

_____

_____

_____

20. How have you learned the "business basics" of the job?

_____

_____

_____

_____

_____

21. Tips on learning the "business basics" for aspiring and/or new superintendents?

_____

_____

_____

_____

_____

22. For the application paperwork and subsequent interviews for the superintendency, what have you done to enhance your candidacy for the superintendency?

_____

_____

_____

_____

23. Tips on the paperwork (résumé, references, etc.) and interview skills?

_____

_____

_____

_____

_____

24. What can others learn from your successes?

_____

_____

_____

_____

_____

25. Why do you do what you do?

_____

_____

_____

_____

_____

26. Has being a superintendent changed you in any way?

_____

_____

_____

_____

_____

27. To whom do you go for advice or counsel?

_____

_____

_____

_____

28. While we recognize that every superintendency has its own specific set of circumstances, what observations would you make about who is successful and who is not in this job?

_____

_____

_____

_____

_____

29. Can we use your name in our research/writing?
    Yes _____ No _____

30. Future Research—contact with BOE member (hiring)?
    Yes _____ No _____

[revised 6/06]

Appendix B

CODE OF ETHICS: AASA'S STATEMENT OF ETHICS FOR EDUCATIONAL LEADERS

An educational leader's professional conduct must conform to an ethical code of behavior, and the code must set high standards for all educational leaders. The educational leader provides professional leadership across the district and also across the community. This responsibility requires the leader to maintain standards of exemplary professional conduct while recognizing that his or her actions will be viewed and appraised by the community, professional associates, and students.

The educational leader acknowledges that he or she serves the schools and community by providing equal educational opportunities to each and every child. The work of the leader must emphasize accountability and results, increased student achievement, and high expectations for each and every student.

To these ends, the educational leader subscribes to the following statements of standards. The educational leader:

1. Makes the education and well-being of students the fundamental value of all decision making.
2. Fulfills all professional duties with honesty and integrity and always acts in a trustworthy and responsible manner.

3. Supports the principle of due process and protects the civil and human rights of all individuals.
4. Implements local, state, and national laws.
5. Advises the school board and implements the board's policies and administrative rules and regulations.
6. Pursues appropriate measures to correct those laws, policies, and regulations that are not consistent with sound educational goals or that are not in the best interest of children.
7. Avoids using his/her position for personal gain through political, social, religious, economic, or other influences.
8. Accepts academic degrees or professional certification only from accredited institutions.
9. Maintains the standards and seeks to improve the effectiveness of the profession through research and continuing professional development.
10. Honors all contracts until fulfillment, release, or dissolution mutually agreed upon by all parties.
11. Accepts responsibility and accountability for one's own actions and behaviors.
12. Commits to serving others above self.

—Adopted by the AASA Governing Board, March 1, 2007

Appendix C

AFFILIATED ASSOCIATIONS EXECUTIVE DIRECTORS ROSTER

ALABAMA
Susan L. Lockwood
Executive Director
School Superintendents of Alabama
400 South Union
Montgomery, AL 36104
(334) 262-0014
Fax: (334) 262-0344
susan@ssaonline.org

ALASKA
Mary A. Francis
Executive Director
Alaska Association of School Administrators
326 Fourth Street, Suite 404
Juneau, AK 99801-1101
(907) 586-9702
Fax: (907) 586-5879
mary-acsa@gci.net

ARIZONA
Roger L. Short
Executive Director
Arizona School Administrators
1910 West Washington Street
Phoenix, AZ 85009-5209
(602) 252-0361
Fax: (602) 252-8862
rshort@azsa.org

ARKANSAS
Tom W. Kimbrell
Executive Director
Arkansas Association of Educational Administrators
815 Bishop
Little Rock, AR 72202
(501) 372-1691
Fax: (501) 372-2807
t.kimbrell@aaea.k12.ar.us

CALIFORNIA
Robert E. Wells
Executive Director
Association of California School Administrators
1029 J Street, Suite 500
Sacramento, CA 95814
(916) 444-3216
Fax: (916) 444-3739
bwells@acsa.org

COLORADO
John C. Hefty
Executive Director
Colorado Association of School Executives
4101 South Bannock Street
Englewood, CO 80110

(303) 762-8762
Fax: (303) 762-8697
jhefty@co-case.org

CONNECTICUT
David J. Calchera
Interim Executive Director
Connecticut Association of Public School Superintendents
26 Caya Avenue
West Hartford, CT 06110-1186
(860) 933-2066
dcalchera@charter.net

DELAWARE
Scott Reihm
Executive Director
Delaware Association of School Administrators
860 Silver Lake Blvd., Suite 150
Dover, DE 19904
(302) 674-0630
Fax: (302) 674-8305
sreihm@edasa.org

FLORIDA
FL-FADSS
William J. Montford, III
Executive Director
Florida Association of District School Superintendents
208 South Monroe Street
Tallahassee, FL 32301
(850) 222-2280
Fax: (850) 921-5273
bmontford@fadss.org

FL-FASA
Jim Warford
Executive Director

Florida Association of School Administrators
206-B South Monroe Street
Tallahassee, FL 32301
(850) 224-3626
Fax: (850) 224-3892
jwarford@fasa.net

GEORGIA
Herbert W. Garrett
Executive Director
Georgia School Superintendents Association
Georgia State University
Atlanta, GA 30302-3980
(404) 413-8135
Fax: (404) 413-8136
hwgarrett@gsu.edu

IDAHO
Rob Winslow
Executive Director
Idaho Association of School Administrators
777 South Latah
Boise, ID 83705
(208) 345-1171
Fax: (208) 345-1172
rob.winslow@idschadm.org

ILLINOIS
S. Brent Clark
Executive Director
Illinois Association of School Administrators
2648 Beechler Court
Springfield, IL 62703-7305
(217) 753-2213
Fax: (217) 753-2240
clark@iasaedu.org

INDIANA
John G. Ellis
Executive Director
Indiana Association of Public School Superintendents
One North Capitol, Suite 1215
Indianapolis, IN 46204
(317) 639-0336
Fax: (317) 639-3591
jellis@iapss-in.org

IOWA
Daniel H. Smith
Executive Director
School Administrators of Iowa
12199 Stratford Drive
Clive, IA 50325
(515) 267-1115
Fax: (515) 267-1066
dsmith@sai-iowa.org

KANSAS
Cheryl Semmel
Executive Director
United School Administrators of Kansas
515 South Kansas Avenue, Suite 201
Topeka, KS 66603
(785) 232-6566
Fax: (785) 232-9776
csemmel@usa-ks.org

KENTUCKY
V. Wayne Young
Executive Director
Kentucky Association of School Administrators
152 Consumer Lane
Frankfort, KY 40601-8489
(502) 875-3411

Fax: (502) 875-4634
wayne@kasa.org

LOUISIANA
J. Rogers Pope
Executive Director
Louisiana Association of School Executives
7290 Enterprise
Denham Springs, LA 70726
(225) 791-0365
Fax: (225) 791-9140
jrpope@cox.net

MAINE
Sandra J. MacArthur
Executive Director
Maine School Superintendents Association
49 Community Drive
Augusta, ME 04332
(207) 622-3473
Fax: (207) 626-2968
smacarthur@msmaweb.com

MARYLAND
James J. Lupis, Jr.
Executive Director
Public School Superintendents Association of Maryland
207 Pondview Court
Chestertown, MD 21620
(410) 778-0481
Fax: (410) 778-4749
jimlupis@hpiug.org

MASSACHUSETTS
Thomas A. Scott
Executive Director

Massachusetts Association of School Superintendents
758A Marrett Road
Lexington, MA 02421
(781) 541-5098
Fax: (781) 541-5534
scott@massupt.org

MICHIGAN
William H. Mayes
Executive Director
Michigan Association of School Administrators
1001 Centennial Way, Suite 300
Lansing, MI 48917-9279
(517) 327-5910
Fax: (517) 327-0771
wmayes@gomasa.org

MINNESOTA
Charles E. Kyte
Executive Director
Minnesota Association of School Administrators
1884 Como Avenue
St. Paul, MN 55108
(651) 645-6272
Fax: (651) 645-7518
ckyte@mnasa.org

MISSISSIPPI
Anna P. Hurt
Executive Director
Mississippi Association of School Administrators
1601 Girvan Court
Ocean Springs, MS 39564
(228) 760-0241
Fax: (601) 924-7498
masadirector@aol.com

MISSOURI
Roger Kurtz
Executive Director
Missouri Association of School Administrators
3550 Amazonas Drive
Jefferson City, MO 65109-5716
(573) 638-4825
Fax: (573) 556-6270
roger.kurtz@mcsa.org

MONTANA
Darrell C. Rud
Executive Director
Montana Association of School Superintendents
900 North Montana Avenue, Ste. A-4
Helena, MT 59601
(406) 442-2510
Fax: (406) 442-2518
samdr@sammt.org

NEBRASKA
Michael S. Dulaney
Executive Director
Nebraska Council of School Administrators
455 South 11th Street, Suite A
Lincoln, NE 68508
(402) 476-8055
Fax: (402) 476-7740
mike@ncsa.org

NEVADA
Ralph L. Cadwallader
Executive Director
Nevada Association of School Administrators
P. O. Box 371071
Las Vegas, NV 89137
(702) 233-6623

Fax: (702) 233-5794
cadw11@earthlink.net

NEW HAMPSHIRE
Mark V. Joyce
Executive Director
New Hampshire School Administrators Association
46 Donovan St. Suite 3
Concord, NH 03301-2624
(603) 225-3230
Fax: (603) 225-3225
mark@nhsaa.org

NEW JERSEY
Richard G. Bozza
Executive Director
New Jersey Association of School Administrators
920 West State Street
Trenton, NJ 08618
(609) 599-2900
Fax: (609) 599-9359
rbozza@njasa.net

NEW MEXICO
Thomas Sullivan
Executive Director
New Mexico Coalition of School Administrators
Univ. of N.M.-College of Ed MSCO5 3040
Albuquerque, NM 87131
(505) 277-6985
Fax: (505) 277-5496
nmcsa@unm.edu

NEW YORK
Thomas L. Rogers
Executive Director

New York State Council of School Superintendents
7 Elk Street - 3rd Floor
Albany, NY 12207-1002
(518) 449-1063
Fax: (518) 426-2229
tom@nyscoss.org

NORTH CAROLINA
William R. McNeal, Jr.
Executive Director
North Carolina Association of School Administrators
P.O. Box 27711
Raleigh, NC 27611
(919) 828-1426
Fax: (919) 828-6099
bmcneal@ncasa.net

NORTH DAKOTA
M. Douglas Johnson
Executive Director
North Dakota Association of School Administrators
121 East Rosser Avenue
Bismarck, ND 58501
(701) 258-3022
Fax: (701) 258-9826
doug.johnson@ndcel.org

OHIO
Jerry L. Klenke
Executive Director
Buckeye Association of School Administrators
8050 North High Street, Suite 150
Columbus, OH 43235-6486
(614) 846-4080
Fax: (614) 846-4081
klenke@basa-ohio.org

OKLAHOMA
Randall K. Raburn
Executive Director
Oklahoma Association of School Administrators
2901 Lincoln Boulevard
Oklahoma City, OK 73105
(405) 524-1191
Fax: (405) 524-1196
raburn@ccosa.org

OREGON
W. Kent Hunsaker
Executive Director
Confederation of Oregon School Administrators
707 13th Street, S. E.
Salem, OR 97301
(503) 581-3141
Fax: (503) 581-9840
kent@cosa.k12.or.us

PENNSYLVANIA
Stinson W. Stroup
Executive Director
Pennsylvania Association of School Administrators
2579 Interstate Drive
Harrisburg, PA 17110
(717) 540-4448
Fax: (717) 540-4405
stinson@pasa-net.org

RHODE ISLAND
John L. Pini
Executive Director
Rhode Island School Superintendent Association
RI College Campus, Building 6
Providence, RI 02908-1924

(401) 272-9811
Fax: (401) 272-9834
jlpin@cox.net

SOUTH CAROLINA
Molly M. Spearman
Executive Director
South Carolina Association of School Administrators
121 Westpark Boulevard
Columbia, SC 29210
(803) 798-8380
Fax: (803) 731-8429
molly@scasa.org

SOUTH DAKOTA
John E. Pedersen
Executive Director
School Administrators of South Dakota
306 East Capitol, Suite 150
Pierre, SD 57501
(605) 773-2525
Fax: (605) 773-2520
john.pedersen@sasd.org

TENNESSEE
Keith D. Brewer
Executive Director
Tennessee Organization of School Superintendents
501 Union Street
Nashville, TN 37210
(615) 254-1955
Fax: (615) 254-7983
keith@k12tn.net

TEXAS
Johnny L. Veselka
Executive Director

Texas Association of School Administrators
406 East 11th Street
Austin, TX 78701
(512) 477-6361
Fax: (512) 482-8658
jveselka@tasanet.org

UTAH
Steven H. Peterson
Executive Director
Utah School Superintendents Association
860 East 9085 South
Sandy, UT 84094
(801) 566-1207
Fax: (801) 561-4579
speterson@usba.cc

VERMONT
Jeffrey D. Francis
Executive Director
Vermont Superintendents Association
2 Prospect Street, Suite 2
Montpelier, VT 05602-3555
(802) 229-5834
Fax: (802) 229-4739
jfrancis@vtvsa.org

VIRGINIA
Alfred R. Butler, IV
Executive Director
Virginia Association of School Superintendents
405 Emmet Street
Charlottesville, VA 22904-4265
(434) 924-0862
arb6n@virginia.edu

WASHINGTON
Paul W. Rosier
Executive Director
Washington Association of School Administrators
825 5th Avenue, S. E.
Olympia, WA 98501
(360) 943-5717
Fax: (360) 352-2043
prosier@wasa-oly.org

WISCONSIN
Miles E. Turner
Executive Director
Wisconsin Association of School District Administrators
4797 Hayes Road
Madison, WI 53704-3288
(608) 242-1090
Fax: (608) 242-1290
mturner@wasda.org

WEST VIRGINIA
Martha D. Dean
Executive Director
West Virginia Association of School Administrators
100 Angus Peyton Drive
South Charleston, WV 25303
(800) 642-9842
Fax: (304) 746-1942
mdean@wvasa.org

WYOMING
Dan D. Stephan
Executive Director
Wyoming Association of School Administrators
2323 Pioneer Avenue
Cheyenne, WY 82001
(307) 631-9010

Fax: (307) 634-1114
danstephan@bresnan.net

CANADA
Frank J. Kelly
Executive Director
Canadian Association of School Administrators
1123 Glenashton Drive
Oakville, ON L6H 5M1
Canada
(905) 845-2345
Fax: (905) 845-2044
frank_kelly@opsoa.org

AAIE
Everett E. McGlothlin
Executive Director
Association for the Advancement of International Education
Sheridan College
Sheridan, WY 82801-1500
(307) 674-6446
Fax: (307) 674-7205
emac@fiberpipe.net

NEASS
Herbert W. Levine
Executive Director
New England Association of School Superintendents
14 Hamilton Road
Peabody, MA 01960
hlevine47@yahoo.com

REFERENCES

AASA. (2006). *Leadership for change: National superintendent of the year forum 2005*. Arlington, VA: American Association of School Administrators.

AASA. (2008). *Code of ethics*. Arlington, VA: American Association of School Administrators.

Aburdene, P., & Naisbett, J. (1992). *Megatrends for women*. New York: Villard Publishing.

Alexander, K., & Alexander, M. (2008). *American public school law*. Belmont, CA: Wadsworth.

Association of California School Administrators. (1997). *Survey concerning percentage of female superintendents by state*. Conducted fall 1996. Sacramento, CA: Association of California School Administrators.

Barth, R. (2004). *Learning by heart*. New York: Wiley and Sons.

Bassi, S., DeHoff, R., & Hopson, E. (2004). Advice to advocates. *The School Administrator* (March), 30–33.

Bell, C., & Chase, S. (1996). The gendered character of women superintendents' professional relationships. In K. Arnold, K. Noble, & R. Subotnick (Eds.), *Women leading in education*. Albany: State University of New York Press.

Bixler, S., & Dugan, L. Scherrer. (1997). *5 steps to professional presence: How to project confidence, competence, and credibility at work*. Avon, MA: Adams Media Corporation.

Bjork, L., & Keedy, J. (2001). Changing social context of education in the United States: Social justice and the superintendency. *Journal of In-Service Education* 27(3), 405–27.

Bjork, L., & Rodgers, L. (1999). *Opportunity in crisis: Women and people of color in the superintendency*. Retrieved from www.hehd.clemson.edu/SRCEA/YrBkv1n1/Bjork.htm.

Blount, J. (1999). Turning out the ladies: Elected women superintendents and the push for the appointive system, 1900–1935. In C. C. Brunner (Ed.), *Sacred dreams: Women and the superintendency*. Albany: State University of New York Press.

Bogotch, I. (2002). Educational leadership and social justice: Practice into theory. *Journal of School Leadership* 12(2), 138–56.

Bolman, L., & Deal, T. (2006). *The wizard and the warrior*. San Francisco, CA: Jossey-Bass.

Brunner, C. (2001). New faculty member examines power and female school superintendents. *The Link*. Retrieved November 12, 2004, from http://education.umn.edu/alum/link/2001fall/female.html.

Brunner, C., Grogan, M., & Prince, C. (2003). The American association of school administrators' national study of women superintendents and central office administrators: Early findings. *Women Administrators Conference 2003 Monograph*. Duquesne University School of Education Leadership Institute and the American Association of School Administrators.

Cantu, N. (2007). *Course syllabus: School law for superintendents*. Austin, TX: Department of Educational Administration, University of Texas at Austin.

Covey, S. (2004). *The eighth habit*. New York: Franklin-Covey.

Czubaj, C. (2003). Intentional academic dismissal of female students in education administration programs. *Education* (Spring), 123.

Dadey, W., Brown, C., Fensom, H., Hansen, T., Kinsella, M., Quadrini, G., & Whitehill, W. (1998). *The future of the school superintendency*. Syracuse University Superintendents Alumni Association. Paper presented at the New York State Council of School Superintendents (NYSCOSS) Mid-Winter Conference, Albany, NY.

Dana, J., & Bourisaw, D. (2006). *Women in the superintendency: Discarded leadership*. Lanham, MD: Rowman and Littlefield Education.

Daresh, J. C. (2001). *Leaders helping leaders: A practical guide to administrative mentoring*. Thousand Oaks, CA: Corwin Press.

Education Research Service. (2006). *Salaries and wages paid professional and support personnel in public schools, 2005–2006*. Arlington, VA: Education Research Service.

Else, D., (2000). *Strengthening board of education/superintendent relationships in America's schools*. Retrieved from www.uni.edu/coe/eil/bssum.html.

Frattura, E., & Capper, C. (2007). *Leading for social justice: Transforming schools for all learners*. Thousand Oaks, CA: Corwin.

Funk, C. (1998). What women bring to executive school positions. In B. J. Irby & G. Brown (Eds.), *Women leaders: Structuring success*, pp. 33–42. Dubuque, IA: Kendall/Hunt Publishing Company.

Funk, C. (2004). *Outstanding female superintendents: Profiles in leadership*. Advancing Women in Leadership. Retrieved August 8, 2004, from www .advancingwomen.com/awl/spring2004/FUNK.html.

Furman, G., & Gruenewald, D. (2004). Expanding the landscape of social justice: A critical ecological analysis. *Educational Administration Quarterly* 40(1), 49–78.

Furman, G., & Shields, C. (2003). *How can educational leaders promote and support social justice and democratic community in schools?* Paper presented at Annual Meeting of the American Educational Research Association, Chicago, IL, April 9–12.

Gardiner M., Enomoto, E., & Grogan, M. (2000). *Coloring outside the lines: Mentoring women into leadership*. Albany: State University of New York Press.

Gettle, R. (2004). Developing your personality, presence, magnetism and relationships. Retrieved from www.selfgrowth.com/articles/Gettle4.html.

Gilmour, S. (1983). *Toward a mentors model of the personal and professional development of principals*. Unpublished dissertation.

Gilmour, S., Kinsella, M., Moore, S., Faber, K., & Silvernail, S. (2005). *Barriers and support for women in top leadership positions*. Paper presented at the AASA Sixteenth Annual Conference-within-a–Conference, San Antonio, TX.

Gilmour, S., Kinsella, M., & Silky, W. (2003). *Retaining and supporting new administrators: Five successful mentoring models for superintendent's consideration*. Paper presented at the AASA Fourteenth Annual Conference-within-a-Conference, New Orleans, LA.

Gilmour, S., & Silky, W. (2002). *Superintendent development program*. Paper presented at the National Council of Professors of Educational Administration (NCPEA) Conference, Burlington, VT.

Gilmour, S., & Tingley, S. (2001). *The Guilly rubric for ethical decision making*. Oswego, NY: Educational Administration Reading Packet.

Glass, T., & Franceschini, L. (2007). *The state of the American school superintendency: A mid-decade study*. Arlington, VA: American Association of School Administrators.

Goens, G. (2005). Broken-wing superintendents. *The School Administrator* 2(62), 24–29.

Grogan, M., & Brunner, C. (2005). Women leading systems. *The School Administrator* 2(62), 46–50.

Hammond, J. (2006). *Words of wisdom from successful superintendents*. Paper presented at the New York State Association for Women in Administration (NYSAWA) Conference, Albany, NY.

Harrington-Lueker, D. (2002). Superintendent rookies. *The School Administrator*. Retrieved April 20, 2005, from www.aasa.org/publications/sa/2002_10/Lueker.htm.

Helgesen, S. (1990). *The female advantage: Women's ways of leadership*. New York: Doubleday.

Hopkins-Thompson, P. (2000). Colleagues helping colleagues: Mentoring and coaching. *NASSP Bulletin* 84(17), 29–36.

Houston, P. (2001). Refilling the well. *The School Administrator*. Retrieved April 20, 2005, from www.aasa.org/publications/sa/2001_09/execper.htm.

Hughes, L., & Hooper, D. (2000). *Public relations for school leaders*. Boston: Allyn & Bacon.

Huynh, N., & Nolan, M. (2005). How ESM's pick changes the face of local school superintendents. *The Post Standard* (Syracuse) (June 3), A-1.

Ivory, G., & Acker-Hocevar, M. (Eds.). (2007). *Successful school board leadership: Lessons from superintendents*. Lanham, MD: Rowman and Littlefield.

Jaworski, J. (1996). *Synchronicity: The inner path of leadership*. San Francisco, CA: Berrett-Koehler Publishers.

Kamler, E. (2006, August). The aspiring superintendent's study group: Investigating a mentoring network for school leaders. *Mentoring and Tutoring* 14(3), 297–316.

Kimball, D. (2005). The cornerstone relationship between CEO and board president. *The School Administrator* (January), 6.

Kinsella, M. (2000). *A school district's search for a new superintendent*. Unpublished dissertation.

Kinsella, M. (2004). A school district's search for a new superintendent. *Journal of School Leadership*, 14(3), 286–307.

Larson, C., & Murtadha, K. (2002). Leadership for social justice. In M. Rohland (Ed.), "Educational Leadership" special issue *LSS Review* 1(2), 16–17.

Larson, C., & Ovando, C. (2001). *The color of bureaucracy: The politics of equity in multicultural school communities*. Belmont, CA: Wadsworth.

Lawrence, J. (2005). Board-superintendent relationships: Core values, guiding principles. *AASA New Superintendents E-Journal*. Retrieved from www.aasa.org/publications/content.cfm.

Logan, J. (1999). An educational leadership challenge: Refocusing gender equity strategies. *The AASA Professor* 22(4).

Marzano, R., Waters, T., & McNulty, B. (2005). *School leadership that works: From research to results.* Alexandria, VA: Association of Supervision and Curriculum Development.

McKay, J., & Peterson, M. (2004). Recruiting board members. *The School Administrator* (February), 27–29.

McKensie, K., Christman, D., Hernandez, F., Fierro, E., Capper, C., Dantley, M., Gonzalez, M., Cambron-McCabe, N., & Scheurich, J. (2008). From the field: A proposal for educating leaders for social justice. *Educational Administration Quarterly* 44(1), 111–38.

Méndez-Morse, S. (2004). Constructing mentors: Latina educational leaders' role models and mentors. *Educational Administration Quarterly* 40 (October), 561–90.

Minicozzi, K. (2007). How to craft an effective cover letter. *The Post Standard* (Syracuse), October 15, D-8.

Mizrahi, L., & Gibson, T. (2004). Winning advocacy. *The School Administrator* (March), 10–13.

Moody, C. D. (1983). On becoming a superintendent: Contest or sponsored mobility? *Journal of Negro Education* 52(4), 383–97.

Newquist, C. (2004). *Public relations 101: How-to tips for school administrators.* Retrieved from www.educationworld.com/a_admin/admin/admin123.shtml.

Noe, M. A., Clark, B., & Colwell, B. (2006). *Getting the superintendency you desire: Navigating the search process.* Paper presented at the AASA National Conferenceon Education, San Diego, CA.

Odden, A., & Picus, L. (2007). *School finance: A policy perspective.* New York: McGraw-Hill.

Owens, J., & Ovando, M. (2000). *Superintendent's guide to creating community.* Lanham, MD: Scarecrow Press.

Owings, W., & Kaplan, L. (2005). *American public school finance.* Belmont, CA: Wadsworth Publishing.

Reed, D., & Patterson, J. (2007). Voices of resilience from successful women superintendents. *Journal of Women Administrators* 5(2), 89–100.

Reeves, K. (2004). Advocacy at cross purposes. *The School Administrator* 6 (March), 22–28.

Richards, R. (2004). *Command presence: Feeding your own self-confidence.* Retrieved from www.withthecommand.com/2004-May/PA-Richards-command presence.html.

Schimmel, D., Fischer, L., & Stellman, L. (2008). *School law: What every educator should know.* New York: Pearson Education Inc.

Schon, D. (1983). *The reflective practitioner: How professionals think in action.* New York: Basic Books.

Seivert, S., & Cavaleri, S. (2005). *Knowledge leadership: The art and science of the knowledge-based organization.* Burlington, MA: Elsevier Inc.

Senge, P., Scharmer, C., Jaworski, J., & Flowers, B. (2004). *Presence: Human purpose and the field of the future.* Cambridge, MA: Society for Organizational Learning.

Sergiovanni, T. (2008). *The principalship: A reflective practice perspective.* Boston: Pearson Education, Inc.

Shakeshaft, C. (1987). *Women in educational administration.* Newbury Park, CA: Sage.

Skrla, L., Reyes, P., & Scheurich, J. (2000). Sexism, silence, and solutions: Women superintendents speak up and speak out. *Educational Administration Quarterly* 36(1), 44–75.

Solomon, J. (2006). District administration's 6th annual salary survey. *District Administration* (December).

Tallerico, M., & Tingley, S. (2001). The leadership mismatch: An alternative view. *The School Administrator* (November), 23–37.

Townsend, R., Johnston, G., Gross, G., Lynch, P., Garcy, L., Roberts, B., & Novotney, P. (2007). *Effective superintendent-school board practices.* Thousand Oaks, CA: Corwin Press.

Tucker, A. E. (2002). The changing of the guard. *Vanguard* (June), 18–22.

Vail, K. (1999). Women at the top. *American School Board Journal.* Retrieved November 7, 2004, from www.asbj.com/199912/1299coverstory.html.

Valente, W., & Valente, C. (2005). *Law in the schools.* Upper Saddle River, NJ: Pearson Education Inc.

Volp, F., Archambault, P., Rogers, T., Service, R., Terranova, M., Whitehill, W., Brown, C., & O'Connell, R. (2001). *Snapshot 2000: A study of school superintendents in New York State.* Albany: New York State Council of School Superintendents.

Volp, F., Terranova, M., Service, R., Fale, E., Archambault, P., Brown, C., O'Connell, R., & Cattaro, G. (2004). *Snapshot V: A study of school superintendents in New York State.* Albany: New York State Council of School Superintendents.

Volp, F., Whitehill, W., Davis, G., & Barretta, A. (1995). *Snapshot of the superintendency II: A study of school superintendents in New York State: 1994–1995.* Unpublished manuscript.

Wallin, D. (2001). *The impact of rural context upon the career patterns of female administrators.* Paper presented at the National Rural Educators Association, Albuquerque, NM.

Wesson, L., & Grady, M. (1995). A leadership perspective from women superintendents. In B. Irby & G. Brown (Eds.), *Women as school executives: Voices and visions*, pp. 35–41. Huntsville, TX: Sam Houston State University.

Wheatley, M. (1992). *Leadership and the new science*. San Fransicso, CA: Berrett-Koehler Publishers.

Williamson, R., & Hudson, M. (2003). *Walking away: New women school leaders leaving the career track*. Paper presented at the Annual Meeting of the American Educational Research Association, Chicago, IL.

Wilmore, E. (2008). *Superintendent leadership*. Thousand Oaks, CA: Corwin Press.

Yudof, M., Kirp, D., Levin, B., & Moran, R. (2002). *Educational policy and the law*. Belmont, CA: Wadsworth Group.